40

REMEMBERED

40
REMEMBERED

(The 40-Year History of the Beaver Dam Senior Citizens Center)

Kay Appenfeldt

authorHOUSE®

AuthorHouse™
1663 Liberty Drive
Bloomington, IN 47403
www.authorhouse.com
Phone: 1-800-839-8640

Published by AuthorHouse   2/21/2012

ISBN: 978-1-4685-0092-9 (sc)
ISBN: 978-1-4685-0093-6 (ebk)

Library of Congress Control Number: 2011960702

Journey of Time

Etched in this memoir are the footprints
    of those who traveled before us.
History leaves its mark
    as we look back at a journey of time.
Stories knit together for future generations
    bequeathing a stamp of time.
Happy times, sad times, trips and celebrations
    are registered in this anniversary book.
Enjoy the tales and fond memories
    left for all to enjoy.

Elsie M. Schoeffel

TO THE READERS OF <u>40 REMEMBERED</u>

It is with tremendous pride and respect that I put the words on these pages. The efforts of a multitude of individuals who cared only that the Senior Center existed can only be measured with profound respect. They, through hard work and perseverance kept the Center doors open and welcoming to the older adult population of Beaver Dam and the surrounding area.

Basically, the older adult members of this Senior Center built this Center from the ground up. There was little money at the beginning, so they used their own. There were no programs at the beginning, so they developed their own. They needed more room, so they formed committees and remodeled and kept remodeling for 40 years. They had no operating budget for programs or activities, so they started fundraisers (quilts and Quiet Books in the beginning) and volunteered their time to manage them and placed the monies earned in the Center's own project account.

They developed a Greenhouse, a Woodshop, a Bluebird Restoration Project, the Christmas Cars, intergenerational programming, and developed ways to give monetary contributions to the community. The independence, the creativity, and the intelligence of this Senior Center community have created a multitude of new programs and opportunities for the Center membership and Beaver Dam community which for the most part was and is managed with volunteer time.

The people on these pages went about their work keeping their Center viable to the older adult. They accomplished this with a strong sense of character to accomplish their tasks without need for acclaim or recognition.

It is time to read of their accomplishments and give each the recognition they deserve for what they have done. Take time to read—take time to share their spirit—take time to be impressed.

Thank You Rebecca Schultz, Traci Gmeinder, and Patti Maleck for assisting with my many computer and software questions , for assisting in finding pictures, and for being so gracious with your time.

Thank you to those who verbally provided stories and historical background for the book.

Thank you, Evonne Koeppen, for providing a space for the Archives and a place for researching all those many documents located there. Thank you for writing the summary located at the end of the book. Mostly, thank you for providing the many opportunities that I have been able to experience as a member of the Beaver Dam Senior Center.

Thank you, Ellie Schoeffel, for writing the beautiful poem located at the beginning of this book and for your encouraging words and friendship.

The content of the book came from the Archives of the Beaver Dam Senior Center which included Secretary's minutes, Director's summaries, Senior Center newsletters, photo albums, scrapbooks, and personal interviews. The book reflects the history I found there. It is my concern that some person or program or event was forgotten because it was not recorded in the Archives of the Beaver Dam Senior Center or was recorded incorrectly. It was not my intention to miss you or to misrepresent you. I would love to hear your story if it was forgotten.

It has been an incredible experience, and I am glad I took this journey.

Kay

40 REMEMBERED
(The 40-Year History of the Beaver Dam Senior Citizens Center)

TABLE OF CONTENTS

Topic	Page Number

Topic	Page Number

Topic	Page Number

C

Topic	Page Number

Topic	Page Number

Topic	Page Number

Topic	Page Number

Topic	Page Number

Topic	Page Number

Topic	Page Number

Topic	Page Number

Topic	Page Number

Topic	Page Number

AND SO WE STARTED . . .

How did it all get started—as an idea—as a thought—by a passionate group of individuals who cared about the senior population in Beaver Dam.

Organization for Senior Citizens

The Organization for Senior Citizens group started in the 1950s through the Beaver Dam Recreation Department. Very active with this group was Audrey Benike. Very little is known about the group in our history. However, mention is made of a part-time program for seniors at the City Recreation Department.

There were limited programs in the community for the aged. Most were located at churches and fraternal groups on a very limited basis. All were considered inadequate. However, the 1960 census showed that seniors comprised 28 percent of the population of Beaver Dam—with 1600 over the age of 65 and 2200 between the ages of 50 to 64. The 1970 census projected an even larger elderly population.

Beaver Dam Senior Citizens Organization

Our story begins with the Beaver Dam Senior Citizens Organization chaired by Audrey Benike. Recognizing the increasing senior population in Beaver Dam, this group advocated for enriching the lives of seniors with programs and activities to profit seniors in economic and social aspects of community life and to stimulate public awareness of the needs of the aged. Their first meeting was September 9, 1968, and they met on the first and third Mondays of the month. The group, under Audrey's leadership, determined that the senior population would be best served by a Commission on Aging. They formulated a resolution to create a Commission on Aging and presented it to the Common Council in March of 1969. The Common Council approved the Resolution on March 12, 1969, which formally established the Commission on Aging as a public agency of the City of Beaver Dam.

Commission on Aging

The Commission's had an eight-part mission: 1) to study the community life of seniors and recommend improvements; 2) to review city-sponsored programs/ activities for seniors; 3) to propose and implement activities and programs for seniors; 4) to promote establishment of programs/activities for seniors with civic and fraternal organizations; 5) to gather and disseminate information on services and facilities available for seniors; 6) to conduct community programs to stimulate public awareness of the needs of seniors; 7) to report to the Common Council yearly about their progress; and 8) to coordinate senior programs with state and national program offerings to maximize effectiveness. O.A. Paciotti and Nancy Nashban served as co-Chairs of the Committee with six committee members: Reverend Elton Moore, Audrey Benike, F.M. Sheafor, Gertrude Deniger, Don Noltner, and former Mayor Clarence Arndt. All were appointed by Mayor Alvin Beers. Members Benike and

Noltner were appointed for three-year terms, Moore and Deniger for two-year terms, and Arndt and Sheafor for one-year terms.

The Commission on Aging (front left to right) Co-chairman Nancy Nashban, Gertrude Deniger, Audrey Benike (standing left to right) former Mayor Clarence Arndt, F.M. Sheafor, Reverend Elton Moore, co-chairman O.A. Paciotti, Don Nolter (Photo Courtesy of Beaver Dam Daily Citizen)

The Commission members with invited guest, City Recreation Director, Bill Anderst, met for the first time in May 1969 at the Municipal Building. They met with a consultant from the Department of Health and Social Services to discuss elderly programs.

Community Meeting of Senior Citizens—1969

The Commission members purposely stimulated public awareness of the needs of the aged. Therefore, the members invited the senior citizens of the community (62 and older) to a community meeting at St. Peter's School Auditorium on May 28, 1969. Over 70 senior citizens were in attendance.

Ad asking for senior citizen participation appeared in the Beaver Dam Daily Citizen in May 1969 (Photo Courtesy of Beaver Dam Daily Citizen

A survey provided to the senior community asked for their needs in recreation, social activities, part-time limited employment, and volunteer projects. Survey results of the 84 people who completed the survey are as follows:
- Largest percentage of the senior population live alone
- 60 persons wanted a multi-purpose community center
- 49 persons wanted expansion of arts and crafts
- 49 persons wanted informational programs on medical, social security, finance, and legal
- 42 persons wanted volunteer services for transportation and a telephone reassurance program for communication with those who were homebound
- 42 persons wanted establishment of preretirement programs
- 32 persons wanted education classes
- 28 persons wanted home-delivered meals

Title III of the Older Americans Act of 1965

Armed with the information from the senior community, the Commission needed money to put programs for the senior community into operation. Therefore, the Commission applied to Title III for a grant to cover the cost of program implementation.

Supporting documentation was required form the City of Beaver Dam—Parks and Recreation Committee.

The Commission could expect federal funds to provide for 75 percent of the project's costs in the first year, to provide 60 percent of the project's costs in the second year, and to provide 50 percent of the project's costs in the third year, if approved. After the third year, the project had to be funded through community support.

The Commission received money from Title III in April 1970. The total grant money received was to be divided over a three-year period. We were one of four Wisconsin cities to receive federal monies. The first year, the Commission had $8,000 from federal monies that was matched with $7,000 from the City. The Common Council expressed their willingness to make sufficient matching funds available for the last two years of the project. In total, the Commission received $67,207. Betty Maier became the project director.

And So Began the Search for a Building

Exploration of available sites for a multi-purpose community center for senior citizens had begun earlier by the Commission. The building they chose would have to have the capability to educate senior citizens, have the capability to provide a social setting, and to have the capability to provide recreational activities for the aged.

The Building is Found

The Commission on Aging made a recommendation to the Common Council to utilize the Roedl-Jacobs Lumber Yard located at 114 East Third Street as the location for the multi-purpose community center for the senior population of Beaver Dam. The building dimensions were 50 x 50 (2,500 square feet) with four anterooms (12 x 12 each), two lavatories, and two entrances/exits on 2-1/2 acres of land.

The Building is Approved

A Common Council Resolution dated March 2, 1970, unanimously approved, establishing the agreement to lease the Roedl-Jacobs Lumber Yard as the senior citizen service center. The lease was for three years at a rental cost of $250 a month. The building was renamed the Beaver Dam Senior Citizens Center.

Opening Day

On May 4, 1970, the Beaver Dam Senior Center officially opened.

Any person aged 55 or over, retired, and a resident of the City of Beaver Dam or immediate surrounding rural area was eligible to participate in the services of the Center. All persons regardless of race, economic status, or religious affiliation were to have equal access to the Center. There were no membership dues, entrance fees, or payments for services assessed. The Center was open six days a week:

- Monday 9 to 5;
- Tuesday through Friday 10 to 5;
- Sunday 1 to 5.

The First Senior Center Director

Audrey Benike was hired by the Commission on Aging as the first full-time Senior Center Director. The Senior Center Director was responsible for the direction of the Center's operation and for hiring personnel and coordinating volunteers. Mrs. Benike was also in charge of program creation, program coordination, and all activities.

Volunteers handled the administrative procedures: typing, answering telephone, and duplicating and also took charge of the Center in Mrs. Benike's absence.

Senior Citizen's Advisory Board—1970

Around this time, an advisory board consisting of senior citizens was formed to assist the Commission. They were elected by their peers. The members were: Mrs. Adela Neuman, Mrs. Alfred Backhaus, Mrs. Elsie Dinkel, Mrs. Emma Kenitzer, Mrs. Ella Zimmer, and Gilbert Schindel.

The Lease is Up

In June of 1972, the Park and Recreation Department of the City was enthusiastic about the present location of the Beaver Dam Senior Center for use by the senior population.

The Roedl-Jacobs property was put up for sale in April of 1972. The lease on the building was to expire in March of 1973. What to do?

Benefactor to the Rescue—November 6, 1972

Mrs. Ann (Rogers) Pffeffer donated $50,000 to be used toward the purchase of the Roedl-Jacobs property at 114 East Third Street specifically to be used as the Beaver Dam Senior Citizens Center. She stipulated that the Center be used for educational, cultural, and recreational purposes only.

How a Lumber Yard Became a Senior Center

Resolution 176

The Common Council by Resolution 176 agreed that the City of Beaver Dam would offer to purchase the Roedl-Jacobs property as a permanent facility for the senior citizens. The purchase price was not to exceed $90,000 on a 10-year land contract.

Mrs.Ann (Rogers) Pfeffer's terms were 10 percent down and 10 percent per year ($5,000 per year) until the balance was paid. The resolution was passed unanimously by the Common Council.

Resolution 195—December 18, 1972

The City of Beaver Dam authorized funds to purchase the Roedl-Jacobs property for $85,000 to be used as the Beaver Dam Senior Citizens Center. Mrs.Ann (Rogers) Pfeffer's donation of $50,000 served as the initial funding. The remaining balance of $35,000 was borrowed from Marine Bank in Beaver Dam for five years at a rate not to exceed 4-1/2 percent interest. The Resolution passed unanimously by the Common Council.

Official Closing for the Property—1973

The City of Beaver Dam took title to the property at 114 East Third at an official closing at the Municipal Building. This assured that the property would remain as the Beaver Dam Senior Citizens Center.

Taking title: (seated from left to right): City Attorney David Schacht; Mayor Alvin Beers who hands the check to Edward M. Jacobs representing the owners of the property; and Frank Woodworth, attorney for the sellers. Standing is John Kemnitz, realtor who handled the sale.

City of Beaver Dam Establishes Jurisdiction of the Beaver Dam Senior Center

The Parks and Recreation Department of the City of Beaver Dam established jurisdiction of the Beaver Dam Senior Center in April 1973. In that capacity, the Department authorized the budget for the Center, served as a resource for the development of programs, policies, and procedures, and provided maintenance services and other services as directed. The Center Director, Commission on Aging, and Senior Citizen Advisory Board would continue.

In mid-April, a document called Guidelines and Policy for the Senior Citizens Center was approved by the Parks and Recreation Department.

Forty years ago in 1970, Senior Centers were established as a place for seniors to meet socially and participate in a variety of social activities. The term used was "drop-in" center where senior citizens could drop by when downtown to rest, meet friends and visit, play games, or watch television.

When our Center opened on May 4, 1970, there was no operating budget. Any improvements had to be requested from the Commission on Aging or the City of Beaver Dam. Activities were financed by the participants through their own individual donations or from donations from business and fraternal groups in the community.

Benefit Basketball Game—April 28, 1970

A special basketball game between the Marquette Warriors college team (NIT champions) and the Miller Skelly Service city team (City Champions) was held on April 28, 1970. Joe Helfert served as honorary coach for the Marquette Warrior team; Art Lueck served as honorary coach for the Miller Skelly team. Miller Skelly team members were: Charlie McDonald, Floyd Henschel, Fred Miller, Jon Mark Schoon, Karl Nienhuis, Dave Neuberger, Con Yagodinski, and Don Klagge. The teams played two halves. At halftime, there was a free throw competition and the Beaver High School band played.

All proceeds from the game were given to the Beaver Dam Senior Center. Tickets were $1 apiece and three business owners competed to have the most sales.

Top Ticket Sellers for Beaver Bowl: Bud Jarogoske of Bud's Cozy Counter; Chuck Cook of Charlie Browns; and John Stavropolus of Chili Johns. (Photo Courtesy of Beaver Dam Daily Citizen)

Our history does not say who won the game. John Oathout from the American National Bank and Treasurer of the project presented O.A. Paciotti with a check for $2910.51. Mr. Paciotti, president of the Commission on Aging, said the money would be used for special needs at the Center.

What the Center Looked Like in 1970

There was one large room with a large oversized counter. Audrey remembers there was a high stool behind the counter that was broken. Four small rooms were on the left and right of the main room. One room to the right had a sink so it was used as the kitchen. Two other rooms to the right were a tiny room for files and a bathroom. One room to the left appeared to house the lumber company's office. The back room was a large empty space which probably had been for lumber yard storage. There were multiple levels and there were large windows.

Through donations, the large room eventually included a Library, piano, television, easy chairs, card tables and chairs. A utility room housed the duplicating machine and typewriter. The Director used one of the small rooms as an office.

Front of Beaver Dam Senior Citizen Center, 114 East Third Street: Audrey Benike (left); O.A. Paciotti (right) (Photo Courtesy of Beaver Dam Daily Citizen)

To make the Center operational, people and organizations donated a place setting of dishes, silverware settings, a television, stereo, a movie projector and screen, a coffeemaker, and kitchen utensils.

Senior Participation in 1970

Ninety six people participated at the Senior Center in its first month. Drop by visitors numbered 212. By August, that number almost tripled as 245 people participated and 419 visited—"the word was out."

To get that word out:
- Women called others in the community encouraging them to come to the Center.
- Seniors drove other seniors to the Center.
- Audrey Benike spoke at service clubs and other organizations about the Center—her message was that the Center was an integral part of the community and every citizen should be aware of the Center's existence.
- Adela Neuman wrote a column called, "The Voice of the Senior Citizens Center" for the local newspaper.
- Julia Teeter kept the history of the Center in a scrapbook that is stored in the Archives of the Center.
- Everyone was encouraged to bring a friend to the Center on "Bring a Guest Day."

- A handbill was developed to acquaint the community about the Center which was distributed by the women of Welcome Wagon and in grocery bags in supermarkets.
- A program was developed called, "Seniors Getting to Know the Community and the Community Getting to Know the Seniors."
- Open houses were scheduled to tour the Senior Center.

Seniors appreciated a place where laughter, tears, problems, love, handshakes, friendships, work, joy, and total involvement and concern for one another was experienced daily as stated by Audrey Benike, Senior Center Director. Seniors were actively engaged in developing programs to meet senior needs and had a sense of personal involvement.

Volunteers in the Social Years

Volunteers were an integral part of the Senior Center's success. As there was no hired staff other than the Director, volunteers took on roles to keep the Center operational. In that first month, 24 seniors donated 95 hours of their time. By 1974, those volunteer hours increased as more programs and activities were developed.

Transportation to the Center in the Social Years—1970-1972

Friends brought their friends to the Center by carpooling when the Center started. A volunteer, Mr. Fran Ingres, provided transportation to members every Tuesday and Thursday morning beginning in July of 1970. By 1971, Mr. Ingres was providing volunteer transportation every day. By 1972, Mr. Ingres had retired and a core of volunteers was transporting seniors to and from the Center.

The First Open House

The first open house was on May 17, 1970. The doors opened at 1 p.m. and closed at 5 p.m. A donated guest book from Davidson Office Supply was signed by guests. Volunteer senior citizens welcomed guests and took them on a tour of the facility. Almost 300 people attended. Cookies and coffee were served. The cookies were donated by local bakeries: Bon Ton Bakery, Griesbaum Bakery, Sentry Food Stores, Crestwood Bakery, and Schuler's Super Valu.

Initial Programs at the Senior Center

Socially, seniors enjoyed a Senior Card day on Monday, bingo, potlucks, a birthday club, Men's Day on Tuesday, sewing, knitting, reading (magazines, newspapers, books), watching television, listening to music, chatting, coffee and conversation.
- **Bingo.** The first bingo game was played in May 1970. Participants brought baked goods to give as door prizes. Later participants brought two-15 cent gifts that were used as door prizes. In August 1970, those gifts were increased to 25 cents. Women took turns calling bingo. **Penny bingo—October 1971.**

Participants played for a penny a game and collected for 10 games at a time. The number of people was counted to see how much money was collected. That was divided by 10. That gave the amount of the prizes. A participant could only win once in a 10-game set. Penny bingo continued into the late '70s.

Playing bingo at the Senior Center

- **Senior Card Day.** Monday was designated as Senior Card day. In those early days, only women participated. Typical cards were "500", canasta, and euchre. The first sheep head game was played in September 1970. The first card tournament was played in October 1970. A schafshopf tournament was held in December 1971. Forty-eight people attended. The winning prizes were ham, capons, and turkeys.
- **Men's Day.** This day was instituted to encourage men to join the Center. Men had discussions on farming, gardening, hunting, fishing, or service experiences each Tuesday. Cards were played and an occasional checker game could be seen.
- **Birthday Club**. The Birthday Club met on either the first or third Monday of the month. Members would meet to determine what they would bring; this was only a women's club in the early days. At times, there were as many as 100 members in the Club. Members served cake and ice cream that they

donated until some members said they could not "eat sweets", so sandwiches and coffee were donated and also served.

- **Wednesday, Thursday, Friday, Sunday**. Early on, these days were basically free days to enjoy any Center activities. Later visitors to the Center were welcomed on Wednesday. Thursdays were designated for classes when they began. Friday was "come and do something of your choice." Later Fridays became potluck days. Host and hostesses provided activities on Sunday. When special activities such as speakers, movies, or slide presentations began, they could be seen scheduled on Wednesday, Thursday, or Friday.
- **Pool**. The first pool table arrived at the Center in April of 1972 provided by the Beaver Dam Commission on Aging. Pool was frequently played on Men's Day. Earlier a bumper pool table was donated by Mr. & Mrs. Paul Neuman.
- **Horseshoes**. Horseshoe pits were completed in June or July of 1972. Volunteers assisted the Park Department City workers in making the pits.
- **Shuffleboard.** A shuffleboard court was established in 1974.

The Center Director sought information from senior center participants. After Birthday Club days, Senior Card days, or Men's Club days, Center business was discussed and decisions were made on Center operations.

The Commission on Aging and Senior Center Advisory Board continued to jointly meet at the Center once a month. They made decisions relative to remodeling the Center, purchasing equipment, and determining where donated money and Title III and matching City funds were to be allocated for Center operation.

Refreshments in the Early Years

No matter the day—no matter the event—seniors donated refreshments to share. Popular choices were sandwiches, cookies, cake, and always coffee.

Coffee fund

The coffee fund was started by Audrey Benike with a $3.94 donation. Donations kept the fund alive. Milk, cheese, sugar, cream, and snacks were provided from the fund.

The Men's coffee fund started in October 1970. The fund was used to provide snacks, etc. specific to Men's Day only. It, too, was kept replenished by donations.

We Will Eat Today for Tomorrow We May Diet

Seniors adopted this phrase as the motto for the potluck dinner or supper where seniors brought their favorite dish to pass and shared it with the others who attended. This was the highlighted social event in the social years.

The first potluck supper was held on June 5, 1970. It was "termed nothing but a success." Many people attended and WBEV taped comments from the senior citizens in attendance. The comments were used as a week of "spots" at the radio station. Two staff members from the local paper came to take pictures and to gather information from the senior citizens. Volunteers from the center donated the food.

Potlucks continued as a social event where people greeted friends and made new ones. The main day for a potluck was Friday, but a host or hostess could "potluck it" on a Sunday also. At the potlucks, you could find members playing cards, having conversations around a table, sharing their favorite recipes, or trying out a new dish that they placed on their plate full of food.

Later in the social years, other Senior Centers from Berlin, Hartford, Sun Prairie, Fond du Lac, Madison, Watertown, Waupun, and Juneau visited the Beaver Dam Senior Center. The specialty of our Center was to have a potluck when they visited. Sometimes they played cards—sometimes they played bingo. They always conversed or shared a laugh or two.

Cleanup was a special time—it was made more special when the men assisted. Cleaning up after meals was a social activity where people enjoyed working together.

Holidays in 1970

The Senior Center was open for holidays—Halloween, Thanksgiving, Christmas, and New Years Day in 1970. The Center was open so a person living alone would have some companionship on those days.

The First Halloween at the Beaver Dam Senior Center

The Beaver Dam Senior High Environmentalists group had a bake sale to raise money for the Halloween party at the Center. They decorated the Center, made favors, and painted murals on the large windows. All the food was made by the students. The party included singing folk songs, playing guitar, and trick or treat bingo.

The First Thanksgiving at the Beaver Dam Senior Center

It was called "Sharing of the Loaves." Each person attending brought three sandwiches and six cookies. Each person received a "loaf of bread" donated by Fullerton's on the Lake.

The First Christmas at the Beaver Dam Senior Center

Preparations began in November as Center members made homemade Christmas ornaments out of ribbon, bells, foil, construction paper, fabric, and colored string. A good crowd gathered and several new members were in attendance. They were happy that they had chosen this day as their first visit. A new member made a hand crafted wreath of cones and ornaments which was delivered and placed on the front door of the Center. Helen Bentley suggested clever ideas for the ornaments and headed the group making them.

Helen Bentley gave the first Christmas party at the Center for her Artex painters from her Artex painting class. The members were to draw names and exchange hand painted gifts. However on the day of the party, Wisconsin weather did not cooperate and they were snowed out. The party was rescheduled for January.

The Christmas tree was donated by a local environmentalist and Audrey Benike and her husband went to the farm and cut the tree two days before it was to be trimmed. It was trimmed with those homemade ornaments made at the Center and with strings of popcorn and cranberries. Members at the Center strung the popcorn and cranberries—the oldest member stringing popcorn was 95 years old. He said, "I really felt I contributed to decorating the tree."

A special day occurred when the Beaver Dam Youth Choir came to visit. The day started with playing cards. Afterwards, the Choir members served Christmas cookies, bars, and coffee. The Beaver Dam Youth Choir finished the day performing and seniors joyfully joined in to sing along.

The Senior Citizens Card Club celebrated the October, November, and December birthdays with a Birthday and Christmas party. Prizes were given for all the types of cards played. The food was great.

The last "Show and Sell" day for 1970 arrived in December. Center members displayed their handcrafted items and hoped they would sell to interested parties.

Mr. Carlton delivered an organ for Mrs. Clough to play musical selections. The Men's Day group helped to get the organ from the van and set it up in the Center. One member of the Men's Day group played some musical selections, and the men joined together in singing some favorite songs. Audrey joked that slowly and surely she is getting the men out of the taverns and into the Center.

Mrs. Clough came the next day and played the organ for the community singing event. She played old favorites and songs requested by the Seniors at the event. Mr. Gene Benike directed the group in song. Mrs. George Kurtz beautifully sang "O Christmas Tree" in German. A potluck dinner provided food and all ate heartily.

One member said, "I enjoy the Center better than anything else," providing a joyful ending to 1970. The Center was closed for Christmas starting in 1971 which made 1970 a special Christmas for those lucky to be there.

The First New Years at the Beaver Dam Senior Center

A New Year's Punch Party was held with food donated by local businesses: Kraft Foods donated cheese, Matlin's Furniture Store donated fruitcakes; Mr. and Mrs. Burt Boyer and Mr. and Mrs. Fran Ingres donated additional food. Men asked Audrey it she would put a "stick" in the punch. She replied, "Sure, a cinnamon stick."

Other Food Days in the Social Years—1970-1974

These days brought so much satisfaction to the participants. The Center provided a place to laugh, share a meal, and share an afternoon to combat loneliness. To make small meals at home was difficult, so food days offered a real treat to the participants.

Frequently, Norman Glatzel would play the piano or Audrey Schinkel would play the organ after its placement in the Center in 1972. Seniors would participate in sing-alongs. Frequently, members would bring in slides of trips they had taken to share with other seniors in attendance.

Other food days included: Salad Day (brought salads of all varieties); Pie in the Sky Day (brought a pie to sell or to use as a card prize—played cards and ate pie); Friday the 13th (brought cookie dough to make a dozen cookies—baked the cookies at the Center, played cards, and ate them with coffee); Dessert Day (brought desserts of all varieties).

Entertainment in the Social Years

Groups from the community were generous with their time and came to entertain the seniors at the Senior Center. Among them were: Gloria Wahlen Dance Studio students, Fred Parfrey and his German band, singing school children from first to sixth grade, Brownie troops, Mary Ann Miller Academy of Dance and Related Arts, and an Accordion Band from the Beaver Dam Music Center. Frequently, senior volunteers would bake cookies to share with these groups after a day of entertainment.

Senior Centers from other communities came for visits. The first Senior Center that visited us was the Berlin Senior Center in October of 1971. Volunteers prepared casseroles, squash, salad, dinner rolls, and coffee. Seniors from the Center planned the whole day. In turn, the first senior center that our seniors visited was the Berlin Senior Center in May of 1971 for a meal and entertainment. Seniors from other Senior Centers from Fond du Lac, Madison, Watertown, Waupun, and Juneau were visitors. These visits were special social activities and were the main source of entertainment in the early years of the Center.

Spring Ball in 1972

The highlight of 1972 was a Spring Ball. The Bob Fehling orchestra played and dancers dressed in formal attire. Music was donated by the Musicians Federation. Volunteers were also recognized at this event.

Cleaning Day in the Social Years

Senior women volunteered to clean the Center on the first Monday of the month until 1972. Starting in 1972, the Center was closed down for cleaning. In fact, women did the laundry on Tuesday and then joined the Senior Card Club to play cards. Men's Day and Senior Card Club Day switched days in 1972.

The Weather Policy Established in 1971

The first snow day at the Center was in January 1971. There were 12-foot snow drifts. Below zero weather followed. In January 1971, the policy for closing the Center because of weather was adopted. The policy stated that if the schools closed, the Center would also be closed. Announcements were placed on WBEV, the local radio station.

Candy and Soda Machines

Both were placed in the Center. Profits were used to supply the Coffee fund. However, they were not used successfully, so they were removed from the Center in November 1970.

And So They Learned—1970-1974

- Informational speakers gave presentations to Center participants on retirement needs, ecology and you, summer comfort, Social Security benefits, probate, health care, distribution of property and estate planning, Beltone hearing aids, art of Artex painting, safety in the home, AARP, and working with ceramics.
- Tours. Seniors toured the Library, St. Joseph's Hospital, and the Lutheran Hospital as part of the "Seniors Getting to Know the Community and the Community Getting to Know the Seniors" program. Sgt. Russell Barton came to the Center to speak about the Police Department. The Center Director, Audrey Benike, spoke to many fraternal organizations and groups relative to the Senior Center and its programs.
- Library. People donated books to the Library that was located in the community room. Seniors actively used the books to read in the Center or checked them out for home use.
- Classes. Most of the classes began in 1972. Classes started sporadically and reflected the interests of senior citizens at that time.

Quilting. Helen Bentley sought volunteers to begin making quilt blocks in October 1970. The quilt frame arrived in March of 1972 making quilting a regular program on Friday mornings. "There is something truly fascinating about quilting." That was Audrey Benike's thoughts as quilters first started creating quilts at the Beaver Dam Senior Center in March of 1972. What started as an activity generated into a moneymaking project as the ladies decided to sell the quilts beginning in June of 1972. Katherine Schoeffel was considered to be the backbone of the quilting project. By September of 1972, three quilts were made—two were to be sold and one was to be sold or raffled at the Holiday Bazaar. By February of 1973, five quilts had been sold. "Everyone loved the beauty of the quilts and how they were made," and the quilters' reputation spread into the community. In June of 1973, the quilters received an order to make a quilt that was to be used as a wedding gift that would be sent to Europe. The men at the Senior Center built a bigger quilting frame by September of 1973 to accommodate the orders that continued from the community.

Lady Quilters designing a quilt

Knitting. Knitting classes began in 1971 with instructor Mrs. Margaret Clark. The history shows that this was the first class taught in conjunction with MPTI. The women made shawls, vests, mittens, hats, afghans, scarves, gloves, and slippers. Women enjoyed chatting, exchanging ideas, and having fun with companions. Mrs. Clark would sometimes play the piano and the knitting ladies would sing-along.

A knitting class with Margaret Clark.
Margaret continued teaching this class into the ' 80s.

Ceramics. The kiln was purchased by the Commission on Aging and arrived in 1972. The first instructor was Mrs. Ritsch.

Organ lessons. The organ arrived in 1972 funded by Commission on Aging. Mrs. Schinkel provided organ lessons beginning in April 1972. This class was offered through MPTI (Moraine Park Technical Institute). Those taking lessons paid 25 cents an hour.

Movies. The first movies were shown in December of 1970. Both were an economic and cultural study of "Italy" and "Puerto Rico." Few movies were shown and if shown were educational in purpose.

Chef's Class. In February 1972, this class taught in conjunction with MPTI was for men where they learned food values and how to prepare nutritious, tasty meals. Our Center was the only one to offer this class in the state of Wisconsin when it started. This continued for five years and then other centers started classes also. The class was taught by Jolly Werner, Dodge County Home Economist. Bill Anderst volunteered to drive some of the men to class.

The First Health classes. The first recorded health class in our history began in July 1972. Stretching and limbering exercises were taught—ladies were interested—men were not. In February 1973, an arthritis class began at Lakeview Hospital. In September 1973, the YMCA provided free swimming lessons two mornings a week for seniors.

<u>Arts and Crafts.</u> Several arts and crafts classes began with the first in July 1972. It was bead crocheting taught by Katherine Schoeffel; a hairpin lace class followed in November 1972 taught by Judi Marthaler; a broomstick lace class followed in 1973; crochet class began in January 1974 taught by Eva Schmidt; and a chair caning class began in March of 1974 taught by George Kurtz. Artex painting taught by Helen Bentley started earlier in 1970.

<u>The First Computer Instruction.</u> The first mention of how to setup and operate a computer was given by Gene Benike in the fall of 1971.

<u>Trips/Tours—1970</u>

Trips to manufacturing facilities, the State Fair, and baseball were the primary emphasis especially in the first year of the Center. Trips to other senior centers seemed to be the primary emphasis as the Center grew older in the Social years.

In May 1970, the first day trip hosted by the Center went to Dundee, Illinois, for a guided tour of Haeger Pottery Factory and shopping for arts/crafts at Lee Wards Hobby Store. Fox Lake seniors joined the Beaver Dam seniors for this trip.

On July 2, 1970, the Center took its first trip to Milwaukee County Stadium for a baseball game. Two busloads (84 people) from Fox Lake and Beaver Dam arrived at the game at 12 noon. Game tickets were 50 cents and were purchased at the Stadium. After the game, the travelers stopped at Hartwigs Gobbler Supper Club for supper. The cost of bus fare was $2.25 and the dinner at the Gobbler was $3, both paid prior to the trip.

August of 1970 found a busload of seniors traveling to the Wisconsin State Fair. They arrived at 10 and left at 5. Travelers enjoyed supper at the Sweden House.

October of 1970 found the seniors traveling to Ripon to tour the Little White Schoolhouse and Ripon Foods Company. Chewing cookies and with cookie packages in hand, the travelers toured the Speed Queen Factory, Ripon College, and shopped at Ripon Knitting Outlet Store. Supper was at the Bel Air in Green Lake. Dancing, laughter, and talking continued at the Ripon Senior Center. The group arrived home at 11 p.m.

November of 1970 found the tour group again traveling to Illinois for a guided tour of the Beltone Hearing Aid Factory. They viewed the inside of a United jet at O'Hare Airport and stopped at the Chicago Oasis for food.

<u>Community Involvement in the Social Years</u>

Two major programs at the Beaver Dam Senior Center in the social years provided direct assistance to seniors in the community. They were:

FISH (Beaver Dam People Helping Beaver Dam People). FISH was a volunteer reassurance program. Volunteers called those alone and homebound with no family. These calls were called "fish lines." The coordinator was Mrs. Max Bauer. The first telephone reassurance volunteers were: Lillian Runge, Alma Arndorfer, Margaret Nedoro, Julia Teeter, Veronica Zahn, Gertrude Hughes, Agnes Bell, Lovina Kiefer, and Adela Neuman. They called to see if they could offer assistance or just to give reassurance to provide a break from the loneliness. The hours were recorded—for instance, 155 calls were made in October of 1970.

Friendly Visitor Program. Volunteers from the Center visited patients in the Dodge County Hospital, Clearview, Lakeview, and Heritage House in Beaver Dam, and Central State Hospital in Waupun. Twice a month residents from the Dodge County Hospital came to the Center where volunteers played games, cards, and had conversations with the visitors. Frequently, donated food was served. Sometimes as many as 89 people would visit. Volunteer drivers transported the volunteers to the facilities. The first driver was Mrs. Sue Thom. Emergency drivers were Mr. Kenneth Serchen and Mr. Tom Raasch.

Additional community service programs were as follows:

Sewing nightgowns. A sewing room was equipped with donated sewing machines. Volunteers sewed nightgowns for the Northern and Southern colonies from men's white shirts. The shirts were donated by the FISH organization.

Wisconsin Employment Service for Seniors. The service would contact the Center and any interested seniors could find employment in the community.

Headquarters, Inc. This group used the Center for a short period of time (four months). The Center served as an "emergency hotline" and "walk-in station" for teens with problems.

Christmas Gifts for the Dodge County Hospital Residents. Volunteers completed a Christmas gift project for the Dodge County Hospital residents. Center volunteers decorated coffee cans called "goodie keepers." Each hospital resident who visited the Center at Christmas received a "goodie keeper." Inside were homemade cookies which were made by volunteers. Seniors donated money to the Sheltered Workshop in lieu of Christmas presents at the Center in 1970.

Quiet Books

Center volunteers made cloth books for children with a learning skill on each page in November 1972. The books were made from donated materials. The books were sold as a fundraising activity. The pages taught children in the age range of three to five how to count, identify shapes, tie a shoe, zip a coat, and how to tell time. The cover was a handmade soft, colorful quilt. Some women who sewed the Quiet

Books were Ottilie Brickman, Emma Kenitzer, Blanche Guse, Edith Lindert, and Eva Schmidt.

Sunshine Program. The Sunshine program funded by donations bought supplies such as thread, needles, and baking supplies. The first recorded mention of this program was in January 1972. Adela Neuman chaired the program and was succeeded by Mrs. Alice Miller

Stamp Collecting. In 1970, volunteers collected cancelled stamps that were sent to East Germany for a program to help educate the children in that country.

Social Years Summary

Looking at the Social Years at the Center, the Center Director and volunteers, and the Commission on Aging successfully met as many of the suggestions as they could from that first community/informational meeting for seniors held on May 28, 1969. Our story now moves into mid-1974. The Center is expanding, so our next chapter is called The Growing Years.

SPECIAL STORIES
FROM THE SOCIAL YEARS

A Title to the Property Story: The Eagles Club had also made an offer on the property on 114 East Third in 1973. They relinquished their option on the property which cleared the way for the City of Beaver to purchase the property for the Beaver Dam Senior Citizens Center.

A Free Throw Contest Story: John Stavropolus from Chili John's won the contest to sell the most tickets for the Beaver Bowl. He also won the free throw contest at half time by throwing the most free throws. John did this underhanded. Every time he would bend over to throw a free throw, the trombone player would utter a nasty note causing a peel of laughter from all those in attendance.

A Trip Story: Forty-four passengers boarded a bus in January 1971 to see Holiday on Ice. Ten miles from the Center, the bus lost heat. Later a latch on a window broke which allowed snow to blow in. Audrey Benike had to brace herself against the front of the bus to hold the front door shut. She used the bus driver's belt to wrap around the door pulling it tight to keep the door closed. The record does not show if anyone became sick as a result of this adventure.

A Senior Citizen Story: An open house was given for the oldest member of the Center in September 1973. Dr. G.R. VanSant was 98 years young. He was a retired dentist from Beaver Dam. The administrator of the State Division on Aging attended and presented a special proclamation to Dr. VanSant which complimented his active involvement in his retirement years.

A Gift from the Community: The Beaver Dam School District provided free passes to seniors for all of their events starting in 1970.

A Fishy Story: The County Clerk authorized the Senior Center Director to issue free fishing licenses to persons 65 and older in June of 1970.

A Using the Center Story: The Commission on Aging made the decision that the community could use the Center for receptions and anniversaries, etc. in June of 1972. The understanding was that the users would provide the custodial cost. Contributions were voluntary.

We're Shanghi'ed: A new card game peeked the interest of the card players in 1972. It was called Shanghai. Norman Glatzel gladly taught those that were interested.

<u>And the Winner Is:</u> The first quilt raffle took place in the Fall of 1972. The winner of that first quilt was Josie Yaucher.

<u>Sheep head Anyone:</u> Andrew Ollinger and Ed Gergen taught sheep head in 1972. They hoped sheep head would encourage men to come to the Center.

<u>Politics Anyone:</u> Mrs. George McGovern came in 1972 to promote her husband's campaign. Mrs. Robert Kastenmeier came in 1972 to explain her husband's new districts. Attorney Tom Wells arrived in March of 1973 to promote his candidacy for Judge in Dodge County Circuit Court Branch II, and the Beaver Dam mayoral candidates explained their candidacies in March 1974.

<u>Sewing.</u> Women completed many sewing projects at the Center. Donated sewing machines were in the main room of the Center.

Sewing, knitting, and designing projects were program
mainstays in the Social Years.

AUDREY BENIKE
1970-1974

Audrey Benike served as the first Senior Citizens Center Director. She had twelve years experience as the program director of the aged under the City of Beaver Dam Park and Recreation Department. She had been a Girl Scout Leader for five years, and a member of the Commission on Aging.

As Director, she was directly responsible to the Commission on Aging.

Audrey was a member of the State Steering Committee, UW Extension, Madison, directly responsible for program education of senior center directors. She helped develop material for other directors in workshops and monthly ETN programs.

Audrey wrote a monthly report from 1970 to 1974 detailing events, activities, and happenings at the Senior Citizens Center.

Under her directorship, the woodshop was built and equipped, the greenhouse was installed, and the organ was purchased. A van called "Good Time Charlie" provided transportation for the Center membership, and a new furnace was installed.

Audrey supervised a "close knit" group of people who wanted to make everything positive for the Center. Members were made to feel "part of something important." The membership developed programs which are still in operation at the Center forty years later.

Audrey accepted a position as a specialist with the UW-Madison Extension Programs on Aging after resigning from the Center.

Audrey stated, "I am deeply grateful and proud to have been given the opportunity to contribute to the success of the Center."

THE GROWING YEARS
1974-1980

The Center was "growing" into new programs and activities. Space had become a concern with rapidly increasing membership. No one wanted to lose membership because of overcrowding. Numbers often exceeded the building code limits. An average of 500 people regularly attended the Center activities per month and 1400 visited. A new director had been hired. And so we begin with the changes to the Center and the new growth they promised.

Greenhouse is Donated

Norm Reier owned his own greenhouse business in Beaver Dam, and he donated one of his greenhouses to the Beaver Dam Senior Citizens Center on April 23, 1973. The greenhouse measured 22 x 34 feet.

Norm Reier

In July 1973, Center volunteers and full-time city employees of the Beaver Dam Park Department moved the greenhouse to the Senior Center. They completed its construction and attached the greenhouse to the Senior Citizens Center.

Seniors and others from the community brought in plants to help fill the greenhouse in 1974. The greenhouse was open year round. The greenhouse was used by Center members for individual use—they could grow and care for their own plants. In 1976, volunteers grew vegetable plants: peppers, tomatoes, cabbage, and kohlrabi. Those plants were offered to other Center members for their summer gardens free of charge.

"Greenhouse fund." Volunteers did ask for donations when seniors took the plants for their own gardens. People could "drop in" donations in a can in the greenhouse. Those donations helped pay for supplies.

Norm Reier started instructing classes in the greenhouse on Wednesday mornings in 1974. Some topics: plant growing, fall plantings, and care of bulbs.

Because the greenhouse was used year round, the Commission on Aging bought two heaters for the greenhouse in 1973 at a cost of $500 and $100 installation.

As the greenhouse expanded into more and more activities, volunteers from the Center made a potting bench in the woodshop. A steel door was also added to the greenhouse in 1977.

While Norm Reier provided instruction, Wally Griesbach, a retired mechanic who was looking for something to do, became the manager of the greenhouse in 1973. He managed the greenhouse until his retirement in 1992. Wally was in his '90s when he retired from the greenhouse. Wally took pride in his gardening. He planted, watered, and nurtured the plants with a core of volunteers. He said, "I've never liked anything so well as I enjoy this. The greenhouse is a good thing."

Wally Griesbach

Volunteers nurtured many plants yearly. Their Christmas plants were used as door prizes for holiday bingo. Red poinsettias colorfully decorated the interior of the Greenhouse during the Christmas season.

Many Greenhouse volunteers took pride in growing
Christmas plants for the Christmas season

Garden Plots

Garden plots at the Senior Citizens Center first became available in the spring of
1975. Plots were 6 feet x 50 feet and rented for $1. The renters were able to maintain
their love of gardening by cultivating, planting, watering, fertilizing, and weeding their
plots in the spring and harvesting and sharing the fruits of the harvest in the fall.
Garden plots cost $1.50 in 1981-83; $2.00 in 1984-88; $2.50 in 1989-1990. Each
cost $3 in 1994-96 and $5 in 1998-2001. From 2002 to 2008, the cost was $7; the
cost rose to $15 in 2009 continuing through 2010. The size of the garden plots
changed to 6 x 30 feet in 1984. The rental fee covers the water usage, tilling, and
use of the land.

Raised gardens were added in 2003—built by Jim Rollins and a crew of volunteers.
The first raised garden was rented by Sandy Skalitzky . A waterline to the gardens
was provided in 1977.

Beginning Days of the Woodshop

The woodshop opened in an open space in the back of the Center on October 2,
1974. Originally, the woodshop volunteers did furniture repair and woodworking.
Norm Reier served as the first woodshop manager, and the shop was open from

9:00 to 11:00 on Tuesday mornings. Jason Merritt became the woodshop manager in 1975.

An early photo in the Senior Center Archives shows Norm Reier, Vic Lohaus, Earl Lohi, and Roman Schrauth using equipment in that open space in the Center.

Good Time Charlie

Who or what was Good Time Charlie? Charlie was an 11-passenger van. Charlie was bought from monies from a grant from the State Commission on Aging in March of 1974. The City Park and Recreation Department agreed to maintain the van. Records do not show how much Charlie cost but funds were set aside for $5500.

Many older adults never learned to drive a car (especially older women). Many seniors were no longer able to drive or they could not afford to buy a car. The van provided daily transportation to and from the Center. The free service was provided to persons 55 or older; however, donations were accepted. By October 1974, Charlie had logged 1156 miles and conveyed 1075 passengers.

Volunteer drivers drove Charlie to take passengers on day trips called excursions. Trips included: baseball games, Horicon Marsh tours, plays, shopping expeditions to malls and shopping centers. Seniors could enjoy a day of activity for a minimal cost (sometimes 50 cents).

Volunteer drivers were: Wally Griesbach, Earl Clark, Viola Lohr, Clem Steinbach, Chester Bashynski, Judi Marthaler, Alvin Berndt, Harry Middleton, Leonard Steinhorst, Howard Bentz, Russ Reilly, George Milton, Karen King, Art Burbach, Irene Udell, Phil Esten, Cora Moylan, Linda Rose, Lisa Nelson, Lorraine Dittenberger, and Ray Lange. Alan Blada was hired in 1977 as a full-time van driver. Later drivers were part of CETA employment or Green Thumb.

Riders needed to call the Center before 8:30 for morning activities and by 10:30 for afternoon activities. Return trips depended on the length of the activity/program at the Center.

Good Time Charlie (Photo Courtesy of the Beaver Dam Daily Citizen)

Remodeling the Center in 1975

Extensive remodeling occurred at the Senior Citizens Center in 1975. The expanding population and ideas for new programs and activities triggered the remodeling of the small rooms at the back of the Center. Remodeling included a meeting room, expanded crafts room, a multipurpose game room, and completion of the woodshop. Volunteers contributed their time to remodel the rooms.

Donations from the Commission on Aging ($2200), First National Bank and Trust Co. ($100), Lions Club ($500 from grapefruit sales), and the Beaver Dam Kiwanis ($500) paid for the remodeling. Bernard Zellner rewired the woodshop and multi-purpose room. The City of Beaver Dam contributed the labor.

Remodeled Game Room. Shuffleboard on the floor and bowling machine.
Bowling machine donated by Mr. & Mrs. Frank Sawjeka.

Open House, May 30, 1975

An open house invited area residents to see the newly remodeled arts and crafts room, the multi-purpose game room, the meeting room, and the woodshop. Programs offered at the Center were spotlighted. Volunteers were proud to show off the greenhouse as it was in full bloom.

Awards Presentation—April 2, 1975

On a Monday afternoon, a potluck dinner and awards presentation was held on April 2, 1975, to honor those who contributed monetarily to the remodeling of the woodshop, multi-purpose game room, meeting room, and arts and crafts room. Also honored were the volunteer van drivers and the greenhouse coordinator, Norm Reier. Each received certificates of appreciation from Miriam Simmons, Senior Center Director and Warren Poland, City Recreation Director.

Kitchen Remodeling—1975

In late 1975 and early 1976, a modern kitchen was installed. Financing came from the Commission on Aging and private donations which included the Joseph Helfert Memorial Fund. A contribution of $800 from the Senior Citizens Center Project Account also financed the project. This left a balance of $125 in the account. Part of the monies in the Project Account came from sales of Quiet Books.

Exterior of newly installed kitchen

Norm Reier organized the kitchen project. Kindt Builders completed the remodeling. City workers removed the partition between the kitchen and the other little room.

The kitchen appliances were donated by Monarch Range Co. They included two ranges, two range hoods, two refrigerators, and a dishwasher. A photo in the Senior Center Archives shows Paula Wezel and Jeannette Heimerl Co-chairs of the Kitchen Committee showing off the new range and dishwasher donated by Monarch Range Co.

Interior of newly installed kitchen showing the donated applliances

Alert Team Benefit Dance

A benefit dance was sponsored by the Dodge County CB Alert Team on February 7, 1976. It was held at the King Tut Room at the Pyramid Supper Club. The Denny Render Country show performed and dancing was from 8:30 to 12:30. Tickets were $2. There was free beer starting at 9 p.m. All proceeds were given to the Beaver Dam Senior Citizens Center for the remodeling project.

Remodeling the Interior and Exterior of the Senior Center in 1976, 1977, and 1978.

Electrical Renovation for the Beaver Dam Senior Citizens Center

The Center received an electrical renovation in July 1976 at a cost of $576. This was paid for by the Park and Recreation Department of the City of Beaver Dam.

Reroofing the Beaver Dam Senior Citizens Center

A grant from Title V of the Federal Commission on Aging provided funds to reroof the building in 1976. The cost was $2876.

Fencing at the Back Lot of the Senior Center

The fencing on the property line at the back of the Senior Citizens Center was completed with Title V funds in 1977. The cost was $1089. At the time, the scales from the lumber yard were also removed.

First Parking Lot Completion—1977

The parking lot was completed in 1977 also from Title V funds. The cost was $16,956.03. Sheds from the lumber yard were taken down. Gates from the lumber yard were removed. The parking lot was asphalted and 28 stalls were provided for parking. Six-foot sidewalks were provided along the building.

Pool Room—1977

The pool room was paneled in 1977. A picture in the Archives shows Wally Griesbach and Fritz Heinemeier playing pool in the newly remodeled room.

Newly paneled pool room—Commission on
Aging provided funds to purchase the pool table in 1972.

Restroom Renovation—1978

An extensive renovation of the restrooms occurred in 1978. The cost was $7702 and paid from the Commission on Aging.

Floor Renovation—1978

The old floor tile in the back room was removed and replaced in 1978. The City funded $3500 and the balance of $2127 was funded from Title V. The Center was closed on November 11, 12, and 13 for the installation. In addition, a new front room ceiling was installed. Previously, carpeting for the main room was paid for by Mrs. Ann (Rogers) Pfeffer after the heating was installed in 1974. Additional donations came from American National Bank ($100), Rotary Club ($144 from their food stand at the Fair), and First National Bank and Trust Co. ($100).

Vandalism at the Beaver Dam Senior Citizens Center

An intruder vandalized the Center in September 1975. Police believed one person did the vandalism that included plugging the kitchen sink and turning on the water. The overflow seeped into the main room and throughout the central area of the Center and into the basement. The trespasser also put three paint cans into the oven and turned it on at full blast. This filled the kitchen with smoke. The pool table and bumper pool table were covered in paint. Police believed the vandal climbed through a greenhouse window, took out the hinge pins to the greenhouse door, and entered the Center. No record is shown in our history to show if the culprit was ever caught. The Director's office equipment was also damaged when a scissors was used to damage the intercom unit.

The Jaycettes donated $175 to the Center to repair the damage incurred during the vandalism.

Resident and Nonresident Fees Established by Common Council in 1975

Nonresident fee: A Common Council motion by Fletcher, seconded by VanHaren established a senior nonresident fee for the Senior Citizens Center in the amount of $5. The motion passed unanimously on June 1, 1975.

Resident policy: A Common Council motion by VanHaren seconded by Goetz established the policy of giving a card or button to the senior persons using the Center. This would identify that each was a member at the Center. The motion passed unanimously on June 1, 1975.

Senior Center Policy Changes in the Growing Years

Saturday Opening of the Senior Citizens Center: Al Karstedt agreed to open the Center on Saturday from 12:30 to 5:00 on a trial basis. This happened in July 1976.

There was a favorable response in senior attendance so the Center remained open on Saturdays.

Senior Advisory Committee in the Growing Years

The Senior Advisory Committee was elected by the membership of the Center. Officers were President, Vice President, Secretary, Refreshment Chairman/Treasurer, and Project Chairman. They acted in an advisory capacity on program implementation and Center activities. In addition, an Entertainment Committee, kitchen chairpersons and a Kitchen Committee, potluck chairpersons, and a Tour Committee completed the leadership for the Center.

First Annual Banquet. The first annual banquet at Sunset Hills on May 19, 1976, marked the sixth year of the Center's existence. It also represented the first time that the officers of the Advisory Committee were installed at that event. This became an annual event each spring. Officers that were elected were: President: Al Karstedt; Vice President, Wally Griesbach; Secretary, Eva Schmidt; Project Chairman, Viola Lohr; Refreshment Chair/Treasurer, Jeannette Heimerl.

Secretary Hired at the Beaver Dam Senior Citizens Center in 1975

More rooms, more people, more programs now were growing at the Center. The Director needed assistance beyond the core of volunteers. The Common Council approved hiring a secretary in November 1975. Mary Girard accepted the position. Her wages were funded under CETA (Comprehensive Employment and Training Act). This was her first job outside the home in twenty years, but she felt it was a worthwhile way to spend her time after the death of her husband.

Potluck Dinner Changes Comply to Administrative Code of the Wisconsin Department of Health and Social Services in 1975

The Potluck Dinner Rules: The Administrative Code of the Wisconsin Department of Health and Social Services issued a policy when serving food in September of 1975. Organizations involved in food preparation for sale to others at least four times a year (including potlucks and free meals) must prepare that meal in a licensed facility. When the kitchen was remodeled at the Center, it followed the criteria for a licensed facility.

Only foods in the acceptable category could be served for potlucks: fresh/canned vegetables, sausage meats/cold cuts, hard cheese, breads, cakes, cookies, Jell-O's, and one-step preparation foods that could be prepared at the Center such as: heated/canned foods, soups, and vegetables.

The First Newsletter—Senior Citizens Center

The first newsletter was called Senior Citizens Center and started when Miriam Simmons was Director. It spotlighted programs and activities and informational articles, quotes, and summaries of trips and tours.

Beaver Tales—Renamed Newsletter—1978

A contest was conducted in the fall of 1978 to rename the newsletter. The winner would receive two free dinners. There were 57 entries and Dorothy Thompson was the winner. The newsletter had a new name—Beaver Tales.

Life May Not Begin at 40 or 50 or 60

A multitude of new programs and activities started at the Center in the growing years. The motto was, "Life may not begin at 40 or 50 or 60, but it doesn't end there either." These programs made the Center better, showed how these citizens cared for the less fortunate, and brought about fulfillment to their later years. The Center became a hub of activity for the senior community, and Good Time Charlie gave them the opportunity to take part.

Bowling Begins

The Bowling League began at Maple Lanes on a Friday in 1974. Sixteen people participated. They bowled two games for a fee of $1 which included shoes. Good Time Charlie would transport bowlers to the alleys if needed. Bowlers from those early years included Paul Freidl, Edgar Lentz, Orvil Frost, Harold Schulze, Carl Paul, Linda Schulze, Rose Bashynski, and Sylvia Frank.

Senior Bowling League at Maple Lanes

Ray Lange provided instructional bowling lessons at the Elks Club for a 50 cent fee including shoes in 1974.

Postal Bowling Tournament. Combined teams of women and men bowlers traveled to Waukesha for the Postal Bowling Tournament. The combined team of women and men bowlers from the Senior Citizens Center won first place. The team members were: Wally Griesbach, Alvin Schultz, John Schweiger, Lee Hinks, Clarence Metzdorf, Emma Schultz, Evelyn Kreuziger, Mary Molthem, Esther Hartl (team captain), June Paul, and Florence Lentz. The teams registered the highest combined score to win the tournament.

Rainbow Melodians.

The kitchen band called the Rainbow Melodians started in April of 1976. They practiced on Monday mornings at the Center for their many performances in the community. Verna Janz was the director. By 1977, they received two to three invitations a month to perform. The Melodians had their own special concert at Sunset Hills on May 27, 1977. The announcement in the Daily Citizen read as follows: "Another SPECIAL EVENT at SUNSET HILLS featuring the SENIOR CITIZENS BAND, Friday Night, May 27, 6:30 until 7:30."

The following Rainbow Melodians members were listed in the Senior Center Archives: August Firari, Adela Neuman, Emma Peachey, June Paul, Trudy Fredricks, Sylvia Frank, Vivian Rau, Mary Girard, Jeannette Heimerl, Wally Griesbach, and Verna Janz, Director.

The Rainbow Melodians. Verna Janz, Director.

When other Senior Centers visited the Senior Citizens Center, the Rainbow Melodians performed and were considered the main attraction.

Rainbow Melodians Perform at Senior America Day. The Rainbow Melodians performed at Senior America Day at the Wisconsin State Fair on August 19, 1977. They were honored to be one of the 14 bands who performed—more than 100 auditioned. Seniors from the Center traveled to the State Fair by school bus that cost $1.

Organ Recital.

Verna Janz taught organ lessons to seniors. Each student was charged $5 and the course was taught in conjunction with Moraine Park Technical Institute. Seniors signed up for eight 1-1/2 hour sessions. The students performed an organ recital at the Center in February of 1976. Members were: Vera Flasch, Eleanor Bagneski, Marge Pirk, Pearl Shephard, Rose Schultz, Jeannette Heimerl, Ann Jones, Wally Griesbach, and Blanche Frandorf.

Life Shadows—The First Play

As the Center population increased, new and diversified programs came into existence. Such was the first play performed by the Senior Citizens Center actors on October 12, 1975. It was called <u>Life Shadows</u>, and it was written by a Beaver Dam resident, Emma Nefzer. The Senior Citizens Center actors were: Julia Teeter, Jeannette Heimerl, Ed Gergen, Rose Ollinger, Marge Ehrmeyer, Trudy Fredricks, Wally Griesbach, Joey Haider, Blanche Merritt, Jason Merritt, Joy Neitzel, Nancy Neitzel, and Darwin Siebert. Verna Janz played the organ.

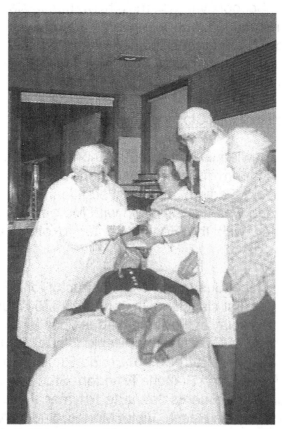

Julia Teeter (on bed), Jeannette Heimerl as the doctor, Rose Ollinger, Marge Ehrmeyer, and Trudy Fredricks as nurses, Wally Greisbach as a doctor.

The 1976 Bicentennial

Norm Reier, greenhouse supervisor, collaborated with the Beaver Dam Chambermaids to grow the flowers for the United States Bicentennial in 1976. The greenhouse volunteers grew petunias in red, white, and blue and proudly turned them over to the Chambermaids for planting. The Beaver Dam Chambermaids planted the greenhouse flowers at the Municipal Building, Williams Free Library, the Dodge County Historical Museum, and Dwarf Island Park as well as other localities in the city of Beaver Dam.

The Chambermaids donated $75 to the greenhouse fund to buy the plants. Chambermaids Mrs. Walter Johnson, Jr. and Ruby Roeder presented the check to Center Director Miriam Simmons, and Greenhouse representatives Norm Reier, Jason Merritt, and Clarence Arndorfer.

Spring Fling/Harvest Dance Parties

Entertainment with music whether it be singing, listening to music, or dancing was highly regarded by the senior community. Therefore, starting in the spring and fall of 1977, a dance and party was sponsored by the Senior Citizens Center. Both events were held at the Wilson School gymnasium with live music played by the "Sounds of Time." Those who were Dodge County residents aged 55 and over were welcome to attend free of charge. Each person needed a ticket. Tickets were handed out at the Senior Citizens Center. Door prizes and refreshments were provided. Dances continued in 1978 and 1979.

Moraine Park Technical Institute Classes Join with the Senior Center

The advancement of knowledge has been a priority since the Center opened in 1970. Education came in many forms—classes, speakers, tours, day trips, movies, slide presentations, book reading, and conversation. Instrumental in achieving that classroom knowledge was the affiliation with Moraine Park Technical Institute. The college collaborated with the Senior Center to offer classes and provided instructors.

- Oil Painting/Sketching: Susan Stare, art instructor for MPTI, taught oil painting and sketching. Her first class was in January 1975. Students displayed their paintings in an art display at the Annual Adult Vocational and Technical School Exhibit in the lobby of First National Bank. Class members were: Margaret Clark, Blanche Juettner, Ruth Staab, Freida Rusch, Charlotte Taake, Teresa Clark, Buddy Wheeler, and Blanche Frandorf. Students were charged $6 with a $3 registration fee. Students Jeanette Rhymer, Angie Miller, Vera Flasch, Blanche Frandorf, Freida Rusch, Violet Mertes, Buddy Wheeler, Sylvia Smith, John Miller, and Henrietta Nielson displayed their paintings at American National Bank in 1976.

Students from the painting class. Susan Stare, instructor,
stands in the background.

- <u>Crochet</u>: Marion Gade started teaching beginning and advanced crochet classes in March 1977 at the Senior Center. Marion also taught rug braiding.
- <u>Ceramics</u>: Loretta Richter was/is a certified ceramics teacher who began teaching her first ceramics class at the Center in October of 1976. The kiln was purchased by the Commission on Aging and green ware firing was free. Loretta provided all the green ware for the class. She had her own studio in her home.
- <u>Sign language:</u> Mrs. Bernadine Snook began teaching a sign language class at the Center in 1977.
- <u>Pattern Alteration:</u> A class in pattern alteration began in 1977 taught by Karen Alderden.
- <u>Genealogy</u>. The first genealogy class was offered in April of 1977. The class was taught by Mrs. Clara Turner.

Book Talk

Starting in October of 1974, Ruby Roeder and Ardis Manthey, librarians from Williams Free Library, hosted monthly book talks at the Center. Books and materials were provided by the librarians.

Cribbage, Bridge, and Pinochle in the Growing Years

Card players began playing cribbage in 1974, bridge in 1976, and pinochle in 1975. Six-handed mixed team sheep head started in 1974.

First Pool Tournament

Pool players used the pool tables for recreation and fun until the first pool tournament starting on December 6, 1976. The history did not mention who won the tournament or who participated.

Holiday Meals 1976-1978

Those alone could come to the Center for dinner on Christmas Day, Thanksgiving Day, Easter, and New Years Day. Holiday meals continued from 1976 through 1978. Frequently, those days would be potluck dinners.

I'm Gonna Bake You A Cake

Seniors proudly showed off their baking skills in the first bakeoff in February 1977. Contestants baked items for the following categories: cookies/bars, cakes, pies, and yeast breads. Prizes were awarded for first, second, and third places. The winners were: Gertrude Marthaler, Vivian Rau, Lucie Haider, Ruth Heilman, Tillie Barnkuski, Gertrude Schmidt, Rose Louden, Trudy Fredricks, Gen Hinkes, and Rose Kohn. A second and third bakeoff occurred in 1978 and 1979.

Meals for the Elderly

The meal program began in October 1975 sponsored by the Commission on Aging and the Unified School District. Seniors 60 years or older could eat meals at any of the elementary schools in Beaver Dam on regular school days. A senior could get a warm meal for 65 cents and could purchase tickets for five meals that could be used at any time. Seniors called the school where they wished to eat between 8:15 and 8:45 in the morning. Instrumental in the establishment of this program was Betty Maier and her volunteer workers.

Dodge County Elderly Nutrition Site Begins in 1977

The site opened at the Beaver Dam Senior Citizens Center on October 11, 1977. Food was provided at the Center for those 60 and over five days a week. Monetary donations were accepted. Those under 60 could participate in the program if their spouse was 60 or over. Reservations were required one day in advance.

Serving food from the Elderly Nutrition Site at the Beaver Dam Senior Citizens Center

Holiday Favorites Cookbooks

Three volumes were published at the Senior Citizens Center. The cookbooks contained favorite recipes from Center members. Each sold for 75 cents and were sold during the Christmas season. Volumes I, II, and III were published in 1978, 1979, and 1980. Copies can be found in the Archives of the Center.

First Summer Picnic

Beginning in 1975, seniors took part in picnics at Crystal Lake Beach Park. Most were potluck dinners. A sack lunch picnic was held in August one year. The first picnic was held in June of 1975 and another in November of 1975. While smaller group picnics were held at Crystal Lake Beach Park, the first picnic for the entire membership was held at Swan City Park on June 16, 1977.

First Summer Picnic at Swan City Park, Wednesday, June 16, 1977
(Photo Courtesy of Beaver Dam Daily Citizen)

Fall Fashion Show 1977-1978

Many women sewed and made their own clothes. Classes in tailoring hand knits and pattern alteration were offered. Sewing was a program activity at the Center. Therefore, a fall fashion show was planned for 1977. Hand tailored clothing was made and modeled by seniors. The models modeled their own clothing or clothing specifically made for them. Those participating needed to fill out an entry form. Narrators and coordinators for the event were Linda Funk and Peg Eckersdorfer from Mayville Yarn and Sewing Center. A second fashion show was held in 1978. Unique to this fashion show was a male model, Phil Esten, with clothing sewn by his wife.

Armchair Travel/Travelogues

Volunteers from the Center and members of the community took participants on travel tours using slide presentations. The program was called "armchair travel" because participants toured countries while sitting in their chairs. Places toured were: China, Alaska, Hawaii, Scandinavia, Iceland, Mackinac Island, Florida, Canada, Greece, the Caribbean, and Japan. Byron Spangler and Rita Spangler toured 16 countries in six weeks in Europe and Spain and stopped by to share their experiences. In the fall of 1977, monthly travel films were shown on Friday.

First Film Festivals

On November 22, 1976, the first film festival was held featuring Charlie Chaplin in The Tramp and The Gold Rush. The piano was played by Sarah Bennett. Movie goers could have all the popcorn they could eat. The festival was repeated in January

1977 when there was a Laurel and Hardy film festival with the movie <u>Blockheads.</u> However, this time movie goers were asked to donate 10 cents. Otherwise, films that were shown were educational or cultural in theme.

First Senior Center Auction

Julius Temkin was the auctioneer for the auction in June 1979. Only senior citizens could bring items to sell. The public could bid on any item. However, 20 percent of every sale went to the Center. The Center reserved the right to accept or reject any item. Items were sorted and placed in lots. Each was tagged with the seller's name and phone number. Verna Janz and Jeannette Heimerl served as Clerks.

Square Dancing

Square dance lessons began in 1978. Rollie Voss served as the instructor and caller.

Day/Extended Tours—1974-1977

A tour committee planned trips for members at the Center. Good Time Charlie or a school bus provided the transportation for the trips. Tours went to shopping centers, Horicon Marsh, John Deere, manufacturing plants, Shrine circus, museums, theatres, flower and garden shows, aquariums, the Milwaukee Domes, the Wisconsin Capitol, Old Wade House, Brewer games, Milwaukee Zoo, House on the Rock, Sports Show in Milwaukee, Arlington Race Track, State Fair, and Gays Mills and Stonefield Village.

First Extended Tour for the Senior Center

The <u>first extended tour</u> called the Florida Sunshine Tour was thirteen days long from February 9 through 21, 1976. The cost was $449 single, $397 double, and $364 triple. Mary Girard served as the tour escort. The second extended motor coach tour called Springtime in the Ozarks started on May 20, 1977, and was for seven days. The cost was $269 double. Small excursions followed in 1977. A three-day tour went to Door County in August 1977. A four-day tour went to Nashville in October 1977. This tour required a deposit of $50.

Senior members were given first preference for trips. Nonresident members could sign up at a later date. At first, nonresident members paid the $5 nonresident fee, but the records do not mention the nonresident fee for trips taken at later dates, so it would appear that they dropped this policy.

Blood Pressure Screenings Starting in 1975

The first blood pressure clinic sponsored by the Senior Citizens Center and Commission on Aging was held on February 4, 1975. Equipment was provided by donations from the Beaver Dam Chambermaids, Kiwanis, and Rotarians. The Commission on Aging bought two stethoscopes and two sphygonomenometers. Clinics were held on a yearly or bi-yearly basis.

Health Programs Provided in the Growing Years

Several programs began in this era of the Senior Citizens Center. "Going Like 60" an exercise program in conjunction with the YMCA and Kiwanis included gym exercise, range of movement, circulatory exercises, hydrotherapy, and free swimming. On Thursday morning beginning in 1977, there was a fitness class offered at the Center. This program was unique in that they were only "cold weather" exercisers—they took the summer off. The YMCA offered an aqua exercise class in the winter of 1980.

Benefits Specialist Starts in 1978

Myra Kaiser started as the first benefits specialist in January 1978.

Sheltered Workshop "Sharing Your Skills" Program

The Beaver Dam senior citizens in conjunction with the Dodge County Sheltered Workshop participated together in a program called, "Sharing Your Skills Program." This program started in 1975. Clients from the Sheltered Workshop came to the Center where senior volunteers partnered with them to teach and share their skills in sewing and crafting. Sheltered Workshop clients regularly came to the Center on Wednesday. A Christmas party with the Sheltered Workshop clients occurred at Sunset Hills on December 17, 1976.

First Senior Citizens Activities Account—1979

Now that the "growing years" have been reviewed, we recognize that the Center was starting to generate money. An account for that earned money needed to be started and in 1979, an account called the Senior Citizens Activities Account began. All money deposited in this account was managed by Theresa Bellone, Director. All checks were to be co-signed by the President and Secretary of the Advisory Committee.

Guidelines for Advisory Board Formulated in 1979

Guidelines were set up for the officers on the Advisory Board in February 1979 President, Vice President, and Secretary). The Advisory Committee would have one or two members at large. Written guidelines for the officers (President, Vice President, and Secretary), the members at large, and the chairpersons of committees were formulated. Three committees were formed—Refreshment, Project, and Tour. The Board instituted a policy for the first Friday of the month in 1976. This was called a drop-in day. In the morning, the Board established a Welcome Committee that took seniors on tours of the Center. At 1:30, the Board welcomed visitors to voice concerns about the Center with the Advisory Board.

Summary of the Growing Years

Wow! The Growing Years were just that. Three directors (Audrey Benike, Miriam Simmons, and Theresa Bellone) put their stamp on the expansion of programs and activities. The Advisory Board at the Center defined their purpose and offered the Center members the opportunity to help the Center with their input and ideas. Volunteer coordinators in the kitchen, woodshop, greenhouse, entertainment, and tours created new areas of interest which Center members quickly joined. Members must have had a challenge to participate in all the opportunities available to them at the Center. The Center has experienced a growth spurt. A dedication to purpose is ahead.

HONORING ANN (ROGERS) PFEFFER

Much discussion took place as to how to honor Mrs. Ann (Rogers) Pfeffer for her generous donation to establish the Senior Citizens Center. Finally, it was agreed to present a plaque to her at a ceremony in March of 1975. During the ceremony, the plaque was placed on the wall at the Center where it still resides. The plaque cost $42.19 and seniors from the Center helped to pay for the cost with donations of 50 cents apiece. The plaque read, "In recognition and appreciation to our patron and benefactor Ann (Rogers) Pfeffer for her unselfish generosity and support."

Members in attendance were Al Karstedt, Advisory Board Vice President; Jeannette Heimerl, member of Advisory Board; Blanche Guse, Advisory Board Secretary; Andrew Ollinger, Advisory Board President; Eva Schmidt, Program Treasurer; Ed Gergen, Adela Neuman, members of Advisory Board; and Audrey Benike, former Center Director.

SPECIAL STORIES
THE GROWING YEARS

A Trip of a Story: Travelers complained about sitting on the "hump" part of the bus for bus trips. Therefore, the person sitting on the hump would get a $1 off their price, but both people in the seat agreed not to move from that seat during the entire trip. All the other people on the bus could move from seat to seat.

Dodge County Fair Story: The men worked at the Dodge County Fairgrounds during the Fair to make money for the Beaver Dam Senior Citizens Center. This happened in 1976.

Strike Up the Band: The Rainbow Melodians earned $25 for playing in the Fox Lake Parade in 1976.

Another Country Anyone: The Senior Citizens Center sponsored AFS student Rodolfo Rodriguez from Costa Rica in 1975. Over 62 seniors came to the Center to hear him speak in that same year.

Our First Booth: The first time that volunteers from the Senior Citizens Center had a booth outside the Center was in 1976. It was for the Beaverland Home Show. Seniors displayed crafts that they had made. Seniors could sell those crafts but 10 percent of their profits had to be returned to the Center.

Plaque Cents: Senior Center members contributed 50 cents each to help pay for the plaque that was presented to Mrs. Ann (Rogers) Pfeffer.

Beaver Tales: Dorothy Thompson won the contest from 57 entries to name the newsletter Beaver Tales in 1976. She won two dinners.

Flag Day: The Elks Club presented the first flag to the Center in 1977. They made the presentation on Flag Day in June.

A Podium Presentation: The podium at the Senior Citizens Center was donated by the Dr. G.R. VanGant family. Dr. VanGant was an active member of the Center in the Social Years. The attached plaque reads, "Donated to Beaver Dam Senior Center IN MEMORY OF DR. VANGANT."

A Taxing Story: Attorneys James Schwefel and Attorney Steve Hannan provided tax help free of charge starting in 1977.

<u>So They Tried It Again:</u> A second break-in occurred at the Center within two months of the first. This time the thief stole $40.

<u>In the Line of Fire:</u> One of the volunteer Good Time Charlie van drivers was a very petite woman who had to grab the back of the seat on the driver's side in order to get into the van. One day she accidentally grabbed the fire extinguisher by mistake and because the security pin was missing, she sprayed an unsuspecting senior who was in the line of fire. The woman was covered from head to foot in white foam. Theresa removed the passenger's glasses so she could see. The paramedics were called and said the woman was okay—the City of Beaver Dam paid for her medical care as well as the dry cleaning bill. The security pin was never found.

<u>A Spare or a Strike:</u> The casualty of the first bowling day was a broken fingernail suffered by Eva Schmidt. However, Paul Friedl and John Schweiger had such a good time that they bowled an extra game to improve their scores. Miriam Simmons participated with the bowlers. The high game was 156.

<u>Special Tweaks:</u> Seniors received reduced rates for golfing at Sunset Hills when they showed their Senior ID from the Center. The Beaver Dam Oratorio Society did the same.

<u>The Governor:</u> The highlight of February 1977 was when Governor Patrick J. Lucey toured the Center, fielded questions, and visited with seniors in attendance. He liked the greenhouse especially talking about growing tomatoes with Norm Reier. He mentioned that the new budget contained several new programs specific to seniors.

Governor Lucey shakes hands with Wally Griesbach as
Theresa Bellone, Senior Center Director, looks on
(Photo Courtesy of Beaver Dam Daily Citizen)

MIRIAM SIMMONS
1974-1976

Miriam Simmons wrote a monthly brochure called, Senior Citizens Center, which highlighted the programs and activities and the Center.

She also started a column with the Beaver Dam Daily Citizen where she highlighted the programs and activities of the center as well as provided informational articles of benefit to the aged.

She instituted the Badger Quiz which asked questions about Wisconsin such as: Which Wisconsin city was completely destroyed by fire in 1872? Who was Wisconsin's first governor? The questions were answered at the Senior Center on Thursday afternoon.

Under her directorship a modern kitchen, meeting room, expanded craft room, and multipurpose game room were constructed. The nonresident fees for members outside the city were implemented, and classes in conjunction with Moraine Park Technical Institute were started. Life Shadows, the first play, was performed; and plants were planted in the greenhouse for the 1976 Bicentennial.

She resigned in 1976 to accept a related position at the City of Madison.

THERESA BELLONE
1976-1982

Theresa Bellone came to the Center with a Recreation Leadership degree from UW-LaCrosse. Theresa moved from Wauwatosa.

The Center was open seven days a week. The programs she oversaw were the woodshop, greenhouse, and garden plots.

Under her directorship, programs expanded such as ceramics, exercise, and the bowling league. The travel program expanded and extended tours and a Caribbean Cruise were provided for travelers. Volunteers increased their donated time by teaching classes, volunteering to escort tours, serving at the meal site, or managing bingo and cards.

The Kitchen Band started playing music in the community, and the Dodge County Elderly Nutrition site started.

The bathrooms were remodeled, the craft room was developed for programs, and the main room was remodeled.

The greenhouse volunteers grew all the flowers that were planted in the parks in the City, and there were 34 garden plots.

Theresa continued writing articles for the newsletter under the name Beaver Tales.

Theresa said, "I can't say enough about the support I received while I was the Director. My years spent in Beaver Dam were a wonderful experience."

THE DEDICATED YEARS
1981-1990

Probably the most endearing memory to the Center is the volunteer who devotes his/her purpose to the betterment of the Center, to the betterment of the community, or to the betterment of the individual spirit. Those experiences filled the dedicated years.

Annual Bazaar

The Bazaar was a major fundraising event for close to 25 years. The event required meticulous planning and was divided into many sections requiring many chairs as well as an overall chair. The women and men who dedicated their volunteer hours year after year to creating, setting up, and putting on the annual bazaar had a true purpose and added many dollars to the Center's project account. As the Bazaar changed purpose and direction over the years, dedicated individuals worked together in exuberance to make each year's event successful. Although the Bazaar began in 1972, it belongs in this section because of the dedication of its volunteers.

The first bazaar was held at Christmas. Seniors made homemade items and sold them to supplement their income. However, the quilters group at the Center made a homemade quilt. They sold the quilt as a fundraiser at that first bazaar. Little did they know that this would start a 30-year tradition.

1987 Quilt—Rosa Kohn winner

1988 Quilt with Ruth Heilman

1989 Quilt

1992 Quilt with Viola Lohr

The quilt was initially made by the quilters group. When this group disbanded, individuals made the quilts and donated them to the Bazaar. The first recorded income from quilt sales was $61.75 in 1973. By 1977, the quilt sales made $341.05.

Joan Brueckman, Doris Schumacher, Eloise Barnett, Loretta Kasper
preparing the quilt for the Bazaar 1996

Raffle Tickets. History does not record the exact year, but a raffle with multiple door prizes (donated by local merchants) was believed to have begun in the 1980s. The raffle tickets sold for $1 apiece or 6 for $5. The quilt continued to be the grand prize on the raffle until 2001 when a Terrill Knaack print was raffled. The quilt re-emerged as the grand prize at the 2002 bazaar and was then retired.

The grand prize turned to a gas coupon and cash in later years, but the raffle served as a major fundraiser for the Center until 2007.

Chili Lunch. Handcrafted items were always part of the bazaar until its later years. As the years progressed, a bake sale, woodworking items, and plants were added. In 1976, the chili lunch was started. Volunteers would prepare the chili, and bowls of chili would be sold at a luncheon. The purchasers of the chili received a ticket to also receive cake and ice cream. Profits from the luncheon were added to the Bazaar profits. The chili luncheon continued until 2002 when it was retired. The chili luncheon was revived for the 40th Anniversary Remembrance celebration in February 2010.

Cherry Tree. The cherry tree was introduced to the Bazaar in 1980. Anne Gartland served as the Cherry Tree chair for many years. Anne would join her cherry tree workers together to cut paper, cut string, make numbers, and wrap gumdrops in bright red paper. These wrapped gumdrops were called "cherries" and were hung with embroidery thread from a branch of a tree. At times, there were more than 200 cherries on the tree.

The Cherry Tree Wrappers

Tickets for the cherry tree sold for 25 cents each, and the purchaser could choose which wrapped gumdrop he/she wanted from the tree. If the purchaser found a number inside, he/she received the door prize that had that same number. Meticulous records were kept by Doris Schumacher. If a person did not get a number, they had the enjoyment of eating the gumdrop. Proceeds from the cherry tree sales were added to the Bazaar profits.

Most of the prizes for the cherry tree came from donated items given by senior center members. Wrapping of gumdrops was a two-day event, and the group thoroughly enjoyed laughing, telling stories, and socializing as they wrapped the gumdrops. The Cherry Tree made its final appearance at the 40th Anniversary Cherry Tree remembrance in February 2010. It is now permanently retired.

The Cherry Tree and the dedicated workers
(left to right) Sylvia Frank, Sybil White, Anne Gartland, Elfreida Grainger

Chairpersons were needed for the separate events for the Bazaar. Event chairpersons were needed for Finances, Chili Luncheon, Bakery, Cherry Tree, Woodworking, Cakes, and Plants. An overall Bazaar Chairperson coordinated the event. Some Bazaar Chairpersons were Viola Lohr, Marion Radtke, Rita Spangler, Anne Gartland, and Josephine Rake.

(center) Marion Radtke, Bazaar Chair (left to right) Geraldine Keel,
Doris Schumacher, Anne Gartland, Loretta Kasper

Volunteers who helped were: Elda Follansbee, Rosa Kohn, Stan Draheim, Dorothy Poetter, Byron Spangler, Ruth Heilman, Gladys Wild, Freida Anton, Sylvia Frank, Geraldine Keel, Anona Garczynski, Alfreida Grainger, Irene Udell, Beth Ingram, Marion Wilson, Theresa Mack, Verna Wendt, Margaret Braeker, Marcella Berent, Wally Griesbach, and Sybil White.

As the event moved into the early '90s, new policies emerged. Crafters began renting tables for $10 to sell their homemade crafts. Those crafters could make the decision to rent the table themselves or share the table with others. In the late 90s, children's games and prizes were added. Grandma's kitchen was also a new event. Free drawings for door prizes were started.

Let's go through some records of what the Bazaar made: 1985: $1099.81, 1987: 794.97, 1989: $809.56; 1990: $794.97. The cherry tree averaged sales of $120; crafts averaged $415; the chili lunch averaged $200. Let's just say that the Bazaar averaged $1000 in income each year—this would mean that the volunteers from this one event would have made $25,000 for the Center in their 25 years. The impact of this event to the Center was a remarkable achievement.

Byron Spangler and the Bazaar Bakery

Byron Spangler would bake sweet rolls for the Bazaar and sell them by the dozen. The whiff of fresh baked bakery stimulated the noses of all that came to the Center on that day. So many were eaten before the Bazaar that there was almost none left to sell. But they tasted s-o-o-o good!

Byron Spangler displaying his baked goods

Bringing Back the Bluebird

Don Kopff had a personal vision and dedication to restore the Eastern bluebird population in Dodge County. His research showed the bluebird left because their nesting areas were destroyed by urban development. His interest developed as a result of bird watching. This sparked the idea that restoring the bluebird population would be a worthwhile project for this area.

As the fallen trees that bluebirds used for nesting disappeared, Don decided that he would dedicate his efforts to building new homes for these birds. His dream became a reality at the Beaver Dam Senior Center. Through special designs, the nesting box for the bluebird was built by the men who volunteered in the Senior Center woodshop.

This project began in 1985. The volunteers built 300 nesting boxes that year. They increased their production in 1986 to 400 and built 700 by 1987. Over time, the builders built more than 13,000 bluebird houses.

The houses were made from donated plywood with donated nails from friends, lumber yards, and contractors. Those that contributed over the years were: Wickes, Specialty Products, Fullerton Builders, Beaver Specialties, Artic Tip Ups, Evergreen Products, John Deere Horicon Works, and Wooden Products Company.

The bluebird houses sold for $2 each. Don said, "I'm not interested in profit, I am interested in volume to help the birds in this area. With these houses, maybe we'll bring them back." The production of these houses was the Number One fundraiser at the Center in the '80s and earned thousands of dollars.

Don Kopff

Bluebird Restoration Association of Wisconsin (BRAW)

Don joined with Jim Kronenberg as Dodge County coordinators for the Bluebird Restoration Association of Wisconsin (BRAW). This organization formed in 1986. Don would take his slides all over Dodge County to make presentations about the plight of the bluebird.

Governor Tommy Thompson and the Bluebird Project

Governor Tommy Thompson declared March 31 through April 6, 1987, as Bluebird Week.

WISC-TV Channel 3 Spotlights Bluebird Project

Mark Koehn as part of his traveling series spotlighted the Senior Center bluebird project on his television program. This happened in 1995.

WKOW-TV Channel 27 Films Bluebird Project

Representatives from WKOW-TV came to the Center and filmed the bluebird project. The film aired on Channel 27 TV in 1990. Because of this one show, the Center received an order for 900 additional bluebird houses.

Bluebird House Builders: (front row left to right) Hilmar Diels, Fritz Wagner, Bill Schweiger, Floyd Schreiber, Hugo Bonack, Art Wallendal, Darwin Bremer (back row left to right) Rich Krahenbuhl, Joe Wapneski, Don Kopff, Jack Schmidt, Julian Buss, Les Thiede, Richard Koepsel, Carl Petrusha, Al Tucker (Photo Courtesy of Beaver Dam Daily Citizen)

Other Bluebird House Builders (not in picture): Jim Ackley, Roland Anderson, Bill Beuis, Harland Bogenschneider, Gib Brooks, Art Burbach, Rip Cullen, Del Denzer, Merlin Domann, Stan Draheim, Grover Grady, Paul Gurney, Orval Gutgesell, Bob

Hanser, Erwin Heil, Bud Immerfall, Bob Jeske, Edwin Karl, Frank Kasper, Forrest Knaack, Fran Kowalchyk, Byron Kostolini, Heine Kroll, Bob Liverseed, Bill Mann, Neils Nielson, Leonard Neuman, John Polchinski, Ed Raschka, Al Schultz, Arnold Schrader, Harry Schliecher, Richard Schwandt, Bill Spiegelberg, Rueben Spiegelberg, Bob Spring, Steve Suitca, Cyril Vaughn, Harry Wisniewski, Glen Yagodinski

The Bluebird Project Goes National

The television shows gave the bluebird project a national reputation. Advertisements in state and national publications and newspaper articles statewide built the bluebird project. Orders were filled from Michigan, Illinois, Minnesota, Indiana, Delaware, New York, Florida, Oregon, Kentucky, Arkansas, Virginia, Nebraska, Iowa, Oklahoma, Maine, Ohio, Pennsylvania, Tennessee, and Wisconsin. Woodshop workers had increased their production to 2,500 houses annually.

Reaching Out to America

Orders from throughout the United States were recorded on a bulletin board called "Reaching Out to America." The board was mounted at the Senior Center to show where orders had been taken and where they were to be shipped.

Art Wallendal boxes birdhouses for shipment
(Photo Courtesy of Beaver Dam Daily Citizen)

The Woodshop Expands its Operation

Eventually, the woodshop expanded its operation. The workers began building houses for tree swallows, wrens, wood ducks, purple martins, owls, bats, and kestrels. At one time there were 2,000 bluebird, wren, and swallow houses in stock.

Display of Woodshop items in stock

The Lumber Trailer

In 1989, a lumber trailer was purchased for $100 to convey lumber back and forth to the Center. Starting in 1993, volunteers received 35 cents a mile when using their own cars to transport wood. Eventually, the trailer was sold.

The Lumber Trailer with Bud Immerfall,
Rueben Spiegelberg, Don Kopff, and Al Tucker

<u>Don Kopff Awards</u>

Don was named Conservationist of the Year by the Wildlife Federation in 1993. The Exchange Club of Beaver Dam awarded him the Senior Volunteer Award in 1997.

Don's dedication not only earned him honors, it gave the Senior Center national recognition. His creative idea to restore the bluebird population gave volunteers at the Center countless hours of constructive projects. It expanded the project account coffers ($18,481.25 recorded in 1991) and provided needed equipment, furniture, and remodeling sources for the Center. Bluebirds did come back to the area. The Center is proud to acknowledge our pride in being selected as the locality to move this project forward. The bluebird house is still sold at the Senior Center as pre-assembled houses or as unassembled kits.

The magnitude of this project to wildlife conservation is enormous. The amount of money this project has earned for the Center, the hours of work that the project provided to its many volunteers, and the sense of satisfaction for the positive effects of this program are a glowing achievement for the Beaver Dam Senior Center and the citizens of the senior community.

<u>Norm Reier Greenhouse Renovated</u>

The Norm Reier greenhouse volunteers dedicate their time to use their gardening thumbs. They are dedicated to getting the seeds planted, getting the plants purchased, to transplanting the plants, and to selling them. The yearly sales of flowers and vegetables welcome customers back year after year.

The greenhouse was extensively remodeled in 1987. City employees spent 624 hours in reassembling the framework and installing a new Lexan floor. Senior citizen volunteers dedicated 1163 hours to the remodeling effort by scraping wooden frames, priming and repainting the framework, painting the sides, and scraping down 600 pieces of glass. The project cost $5722.42.

The greenhouse being renovated

Volunteers repainting the sides

Norm Reier retired from the greenhouse in 1979. He passed away in 1988. The renovated greenhouse was named for him during a ceremony in 1989. A plaque resides on the greenhouse wall which commemorates that event. For the grand reopening of the greenhouse in May of 1988, purchasers could buy six tomato plants for 75 cents. Popcorn and snow cones were served.

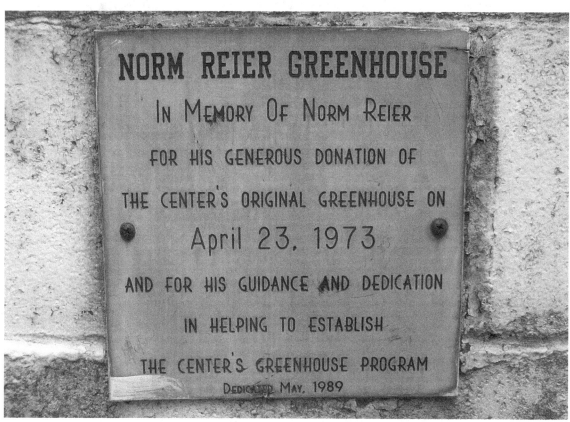

Norm Reier greenhouse plaque

PROCLAMATION TO
BEAVER DAM SENIOR CITIZEN CENTER

WHEREAS, the Parks and Recreation Committee recognizes the fine efforts put forth by members of the Senior Citizen Center in the various fund-raising projects, and,

WHEREAS, we wish to acknowledge our appreciation that funds derived from these events have gone towards improvements of the Center Building, and

WHEREAS, these activities both as a fund-raiser and donor of monies to enhance the Center make for a better environment,

NOW THEREFORE BE IT RESOLVED, that the Parks and Recreation Committee go on record congratulating you on the improvements to the Greenhouse, the insulation of the front room, electrical ballasts to the rear room, and the couch and chair, and express our sincere thanks for a job well-done!

Robert H. Kachelski, Mayor

Sandra Krause, Chairman

Norris Bussie

Peter Jozefowski

Willard Roberts

Warren Poland, Director

November 1988

Greenhouse Proclamation

Greenhouse Starts the Season in January

Volunteers meet in January to decide what they are going to plant for the season. Charts are kept from year to year as a reference.

Heirloom plants such as the Beaver Dam pepper are carried over from generation to generation. Jim Rollins initially distributed the Beaver Dam pepper seeds to the Senior Center from his own garden. The peppers ripened and Jim saved the seed and dried them to use for planting the following spring. He said, "I just didn't want the Beaver Dam pepper to disappear." Volunteers continue to collect the heirloom seed, dry the seed, and save the seed for the following spring planting.

The Beaver Dam pepper was brought to America by the Joe Hussli family 70 years ago. Jim Rollins received the seed from the Hussli family. The pepper is described in catalogs as mildly hot, sweet, round, and thick walled. The pepper turns from green to red when it is ripe.

Greenhouse Growing Season

Volunteers plant from seed or seedlings except for geranium cuts. All are planted by hand in February. In later years, plants were purchased from an Amish greenhouse. When the plants are 1 to 1-1/2 inches high, volunteers replant them.

Carl Petrusha planting seeds

The geraniums come in plugs which are placed in 4-½ inch pots. For years, Orval Gutgesell was in charge of starting the plants. Volunteers claimed that they could plant 500 geraniums in less than two hours.

Replanting geraniums: Mary Hollihan, Donnalee Kuenzi,
Beth Ingram, Elaine Beyer, Gloria Klug, Iva Dorn

The Dirt Mixer

The plants would not survive without a special mix of dirt: top soil, peat moss, perlite sand, and cow manure. The dirt mix specialists over the years included: Wally Griesbach, Alvin Schultz, and Julian Buss. Al Schultz said, "I dump the dirt and shovel it over three times."

Julian Buss mixing dirt

Greenhouse Supervisors

There are many to thank for their contribution to being the greenhouse supervisor. Wally Griesbach, Stan Draheim, Alvin Schultz, Julian Buss, Carl Petrusha, Clarence Arndorfer, and Anne Gartland have made the greenhouse their passion. Iva Dorn has supervised the greenhouse since 2001. Jim Rollins has been manager for over 15 years.

Jim Rollins and Anne Gartland getting ready for the sale

Greenhouse Sales

The first recorded sale of plants earned $277 in 1980. Vegetable and flower plants were sold in 1981. Sales amounted to $1100 in 1982. Flowers that were sold were geraniums, marigolds, petunias, zinnias, impatiens, ageratums, alyssums, coleus, pansies, and vica rosa. Vegetable plants included varieties of tomatoes, peppers including the Beaver Dam pepper, parsley, cabbage, and kohlrabi. Advertisements in the Beaver Dam Daily Citizen informed the public of the sale of greenhouse plants.

Frequently, volunteers such as Marion Radtke, Anne Gartland, Wally Griesbach, or Christian Schultz would take plants to Recheks in order to sell them in front of the store.

Christian Schultz selling plants at Recheks

Planting Around Town

The plants from the greenhouse were frequently purchased by the City of Beaver Dam to plant in flower pots located in downtown Beaver Dam. All residents could enjoy their fragrances and beauty during the growing season. Volunteers from the Center planted greenhouse plants in front of the Center or in front of City Hall.

Iva Dorn and Bev Hack planting at City Hall

A <u>Gardening Favorites Booklet</u> was printed in 1981. It contained recipes, gardening hints, canning, pickling, and freezing recipes. Not only did the dedicated volunteers provide the plants, they also provided instructions on preservation of those plants when they were harvested.

How do you measure the hours of delight a greenhouse worker enjoys? How do you measure the impact of the sales that were generated? Let's say the greenhouse averaged $2000 in sales a year since 1980—that's 30 years of sales or $60,000. We can measure that, but it is immeasurable as to what this program has done for the senior citizen in gardening enjoyment and fulfillment to each and every one of those who volunteered.

Greenhouse volunteers ready for the sale: (left to right) Bill Christian, Doris Peterson, Iva Dorn, Arvid Behm, Donnalee Kuenzi, Marion Gade, Alice Engebretson, Gloria Klug

<u>Beaverfest and the Senior Center</u>

The Beaver Dam Senior Center began participating in this downtown event in 1986 and continued it yearly until 1995. The primary purpose of the event was to have an open house for downtown businesses to showcase their wares. Volunteers at the Senior Center dedicated their hours for this event for the primary purpose of telling the community about the programs and activities at the Senior Center. The event usually started at 10 a.m. and lasted until 4 p.m.

Some chairs for the event over the years were: Marcella Berent and Anne Gartland; Don and Marge Kopff; and Josephine Rake and Clifford Gutgesell.

To make a bit of money, volunteers organized an ice cream social. Volunteers sold cake, cake and ice cream, soda, coffee, milk, single scoop and double scoop ice cones. The greenhouse was also open to sell plants, and woodshop items also were sold.

Volunteers at the Senior Center window preparing to sell cake and ice cream at Beaverfest in 1992

Beaverfest Floats

No, not ice cream floats—floats for the Beaverfest parade. Volunteers dedicated hours to building a float and entering it in the parade. This began in 1988.

Come Join Us—Beaverfest float 1988

This gave visibility to the Center and accomplished their mission of informing the public of programs and activities.

Life Begins at 55 or how many can ride on the float—Beaverfest 1990

Senior Olympics

What barrier is age? How can we change the mind set of the community that we are not old? Well, let's have a senior Olympics. So that's what they did. Dedicated individuals set up the event for the month of August in 1981 and 1982.

August 5, 6, 7, 1981: The first senior Olympics were held at the Beaver Dam Senior Center. Four events were featured—two inside and two outside. The events were: cribbage and pool inside and lawn darts and croquet outside. Unfortunately, the lawn darts event was rained out. However, winners were declared in each event. They were: First Place Cribbage: Margaret Braeker; Second Place Cribbage: Jeannette Heimerl. First Place Pool: John Kaczmarski; Second Place Pool: Wally Griesbach. First Place Croquet: Eldon Elsesser; Second Place Croquet: Byron Spangler.

It was so much fun that a second Senior Olympics was held in 1982 with expanded games and fun.

August 10, 11,12, 1982: Games were held both inside and outside. Games played were croquet, pool, table tennis, lawn darts, and volleyball. Games were held at the Center and at Lakeview Park.

The volleyball match (Photo Courtesy of Beaver Dam Daily Citizen)

Winners were: First Place Croquet: Florence Kelm; Second Place Croquet: Christian Schultz. First Place Pool: John Kaczmarski; Second Place Pool: Edwin Karl. First Place Table Tennis: Hubert Turner; Second Place Table Tennis: Elden Elsesser. First Place Lawn Darts: Mary Schultz; Second Place Lawn Darts: John Kaczamarski. First Place Volleyball: Frieda Anton, Evie Hankes, Rita Spangler, Lorraine Hankes, Josephine Rake, William Poland, and John Kaczmarski.

Medal winners 1982: (left to right) (first row) Josephine Rake, Frieda Anton, Florence Kelm, Rita Spangler, Glenda Bailey Olympics Coordinator; (second row) (left to right) Pat Keller Olympics Coordinator, Christian Schultz, Hubert Turner, John Kaczmarski, Edwin Karl (Photo Courtesy of Beaver Dam Daily Citizen)

Wisconsin Senior Olympics—Let the Games Begin

"Competition is competition and fun is fun. One fun part is just competing at my age," said Frieda Anton Wisconsin Senior Olympics participant. The Senior Olympics at the Center generated interest in participating in the Wisconsin Senior Olympics that was held in Milwaukee. Groups of participants gathered in Good Time Charlie and headed for the games. The Senior Center sponsored the entrants.

Entries were in 50 categories and were categorized by age group. The age groups were 55-59, 60-64, 65-69, 70-74, 75-79, and 80 and over. The event covered five days. There were two dozen swimming events, archery, tennis, track and field, trapshooting, table tennis, and badminton.

It gave older adults from all over the state a chance to meet one another and tone their muscles and compete and have fun. As Ann Neumaier, Director, said, "It proves that seniors don't sit at home and knit all day."

Those that won medals at the Wisconsin Senior Olympics (as mentioned in our history):

- Frieda Anton (80 and over) earned a Gold medal for bowling a 160 game;
- Doris Domann (70-74) Gold in handicapped singles bowling and Gold in doubles with her sister Doretta Romeg bowling a 227 game with a series of 684;
- John Keil (60-64) won Gold in singles tennis and Gold in doubles tennis with Gordon Kotinek. He also won Gold in the free throw contest and 3 on 3 basketball with Fred Miller and Tom O'Brien. John went on to compete in the National Olympics held in Baton Rouge for 3 on 3 basketball, singles and doubles tennis;
- Clara Turner Silver in Frisbee throw;
- Hester Ruehl (75-80) Bronze bowling;
- Lolette Snyder (over 80) Gold handicap bowling (530 series);
- Anne Gartland and Helen Rannum Bronze in women's scratch doubles;
- Marion Radtke Gold and Silver medals bowling;
- Bill Hollihan Gold 400 meter and 1500 meter run; Silver 800 meter run.

Wisconsin Olympics winners: Doris Domann,
Lolette Snyder, Hester Ruehl, and Frieda Anton—1990

Hubert Turner Wins Multiple Wisconsin Senior Olympics Medals

Hubert Turner, Senior Center member, won multiple medals over several years at the Wisconsin Senior Olympics. He won Gold in basketball free throw shooting and Frisbee throw; Silver in volleyball serve; and Silver and Bronze in men's handicapped singles bowling (75-80) and softball throw. He earned 2 Gold, 5 Silver, and 2 Bronze medals at the 1987 Olympics. That's 15 medals that our history recorded—there must be several more for this amazing athlete.

Howard Bentz wins 11 Medals at 1987 Wisconsin Senior Olympics

Howard Bentz, Senior Center member, won 11 medals at the Wisconsin Senior Olympics in 1987. He won Gold in bowling (open division), high jump, and Frisbee throw. He also won Silver in discus, free throw, volleyball serve, and basketball throw. To round out the Olympics he won Bronze in golf, softball throw, 400 meter run, broad jump, and standing broad jump. Howard went on to compete in the National Senior Olympics in St. Louis.

Other Participants in Wisconsin Senior Olympics

Our history recorded others that participated: Al Schultz, Richard Leichter, Ray Lange, Geraldine Keel, Marge Kopff, and Colleen Hein. Others surely also participated, but they were not recorded in the history. They, too, possibly won medals; however for what or when unfortunately are not reflected in the history.

Other Games in the Dedicated Years

The senior community in the Dedicated Years went "all out" to participate in games and physical activity as the next section shows.

Torch Run

What a start to the Olympics. A torch run was completed by the seniors of the Senior Center in 1988.

Torch bearers: (left to right) Ruth Russell, Del Denzer,
Theresa Mack, Irene Udell, Helen Tietz, Erna and Orval Gutgesell

Monday Night Bowling League

Team members and Senior Center members (average age over 70) won the championship in the Maple Lanes Monday Night Open League. Team members were: Al Schultz (80 plus) with a 158 average; Wally Griesbach (89); Erv Schutte (77); Dick Schmid (57); Lyle Jaehnke (59) with a 165 average; William Michel (62) with a 165 average; and Del Winning Sr. (70 plus).

Grand Queens of Beaver Dam

The Grand Queens team members and Senior Center members were all over 70 years of age when they participated in the City Bowling tournament in 1987. They received pins commemorating their years of bowling. Frieda Anton was a charter member of the Beaver Dam Women's Bowling Hall of Fame.

The Grand Queens of Beaver Dam were Lolette Snyder, Hester Ruehl, Ida Grant, Esther Anderson, and Captain Frieda Anton.

Croquet

Muriel Fredrick donated a croquet set to the Center in 1982. Active seniors played croquet at Tahoe Park on Friday mornings. Some members that the history recorded are Bill Poland, Sam Horton, Clara Heidt, Irene Udell, Christian Schultz, and Sylvia Frank.

Horseshoe Pit Re-emerges

The Luther League of the Lutheran Brotherhood of First Evangelical Lutheran Church donated two horseshoe pits to the Senior Center in 1988. Joe Brudahl and Herb Nitschke constructed the pits behind the greenhouse. The Brotherhood also donated bench gliders for the horseshoe pit area in 1989. The first horseshoe tournament was in September 1988.

Golf League

A golfing league was formed to play at Rock River Hills Golf Club in 1984 and continued through 1989. They paid for nine holes of golf. Some fall scores were recorded in the history for 1984. Lowest score of the season, Male: Roy Hubatch 52; Lowest score of the season, Female: Muriel Frederick 58; Most Improved for Men, Hubert Turner 21 strokes; Most Improved for Women, Pearl Landmann 12 strokes.

Exercise Bicycle

An exercise bicycle was purchased for the Center in 1982 and was available for use by any senior attending the Center. The bicycle was in the game room.

It was so refreshing to find these physical activities recorded in the history of the Center. Newspaper articles record these achievements, so the community was aware of the "specialness" of this group of seniors in the Dedicated years—seniors who were dedicated to sports and competitiveness to keep their minds and bodies active and aware.

Dedication Comes in Many Forms

Dedication comes in many forms—in an idea or purpose, in improving the awareness of seniors to the community—in the excitement of planting and regrowth—in volunteering time to provide a service or piece of equipment. This next section recognizes special individuals from the Dedicated years who placed their time to helping to improve the Center either through equipment or services.

Memorial Dedications—Louise Maas, Anne Pfeffer, Helen Tietz

The Louise Maas Memorial fund honored her after she died from stab wounds in her murder in 1986. Members contributed money, and a painting was purchased which was placed on the wall above where she loved to play sheep head. The painting is now in storage.

Jeanette Rhymer donated a painting as a memorial to Anne Pfeffer in 1986. It hangs on the woodshop wall. The Helen Tietz memorial donated $173 to the Center in 1990. Three wildlife prints were purchased. Two hang above the window to the kitchen—the third is in storage. Hopefully, those in storage will be used once again in the new building.

Stan Draheim and the Trophy Case

An accumulation of trophies were lining the walls of the Center from the senior bowling league. Stan Draheim, Woodshop Coordinator, with the help of Rollin Voss designed, constructed, and donated their labor to build a trophy case. When completed in 1989, it was placed in the main room of the Center and the trophies were prominently displayed inside. Later it was moved to the game room (entry room from the parking lot) where it resides today.

Stan Draheim's Trophy Case

Display Case

A display case was purchased for the Center in July 1985. It was purchased in order to display arts and crafts made by seniors at the Senior Center. Those items on display were ceramics, woodworking, and crocheting. Those who sold items from the display case were required to give 15 percent of their profits back to the Senior Center. The case was sold in 1994.

China Painting with Loretta Richter

Loretta began instructing the china painting class in 1984. Her inspiration helped class members create their own works of art. Her students start with a small item such as a plate or trinket box. Layers of color are added until the correct effect is accomplished. That color is composed of tinted powders mixed with oils. Students painted floral scenes, country scenes, birds, or fruit. After that, the item is fired sometimes as many as four or five times. Loretta fired the objects at her home or used the kiln at the Center. The subjects can vary with the creativity of the student. Loretta says, "We paint everything. We are creating the heirlooms of the future. Our children and grandchildren are going to fight over these items." Little did Loretta realize that she would be teaching 34 years at the Senior Center when she started with her ceramics class in 1976. Her dedication has provided many hours of enjoyment and has been a positive influence to the Senior Center.

China Painting Instructor, Loretta Richter, with her projects

The Kiln Firer/Kindler—Frieda Anton

The new kiln was purchased in 1987 for $261.90. The kiln was located by the window next to the sink in the Arts and Crafts room. The kiln required firing each day and that was Frieda Anton's job seven days a week for three years. She said she was tired after that time and retired; however, she still did the task on a part-time basis. Florence Mielke took her place. The kiln was placed in storage in 2001 to make room for computer classes and the tax program.

AARP Tax Aide

The AARP tax program in conjunction with the IRS began in the '60s. There are more than 10,000 sites in the United States yearly. Volunteers with this program attend a training program each year through the IRS which includes classes, book work, and a test of the material. Any volunteer must successfully complete this training. It started as a program designed to help the older adult complete their taxes. It has expanded to include any low or medium income adult. There is no charge.

Our first Tax Aide program was sponsored through AARP and the National Retired Teachers Association in conjunction with the Wisconsin Department of Revenue starting in 1980 through 1982. This is the earliest record that was found in our history.

In 1982, Josephine Rake started at the Center as a volunteer benefit specialist with the Commission on Aging helping seniors prepare taxes, Homestead, and Medicare claims. She did this on site for six years. She also helped people balance their checkbooks. Josephine again expanded her help in 1985 when she assisted with the AARP tax aide program with Estelle Dittmaier and later with Ardys Sharpe. After that time, she continued to assist people out of her home until 1991. In addition, she made house calls as a benefit specialist all over Dodge County. Josephine said, "I think anyone should get into volunteer work as much as they can. They should keep as busy as they can. It's very satisfying being a volunteer."

Myra Kaiser, volunteer coordinator from Dodge County, said that Josephine attended every IRS training session. Myra said, "Josephine was a friend to those that sought her help."

(left to right) Viola Lohr and Josephine Rake

The AARP tax aide program has continued since 1980 with many volunteer tax assistance coordinators: Irene Fernander, Linda Janz, Dwayne Braun, and Rena Hughes. Volunteer tax consultants have assisted seniors with their tax preparation since 1982 at the Center. Among them have been Bill Hollihan, Sandy Snyder, Patsy Radtke, Kay Hodgson, Pamela Sarsfield, Robert Orlowski, Virginia Schmitt, Joan Daniels, Terry Zimmerlee, Diane Follmer, and Ken Weisensel. Alice Engebretson has been a volunteer tax consultant with the program for 19 years. Marion Radtke has been volunteering to greet clients as a receptionist to the program for 20 years—Pat Przekurat joined her recently. Volunteers assist 20 to 25 people on an average day. As many as 650 returns are prepared in one tax year.

The dedication of these individuals who all volunteer their time is commendable. Again, how do you measure this service to the community—how do measure its value—how do you measure how dedicated these people are to this task. I guess you just say thank you. As one client says, "Without them, I wouldn't have known what to do."

AARP tax volunteers (left to right) (seated) Pamela Sarsfield, Marion Radtke, Rena Hughes. Standing (left to right) Robert Orlowski, Bill Hollihan, Alice Engebretson, Virginia Schmitt

The Potluck Can Never Be Retired

Monthly Sunday potlucks started in 1985. Monthly chairpersons were assigned to coordinate the day's events. Each person was asked to bring a dish to pass and their own table service.

Those dedicated chairs were Inez Helbing, Helen Hill, Margaret Braeker, Trudy Fredricks, Tillie Barnkuski, Viola Lohr, Jeannette Heimerl, Helen Kazmierski, Gertrude Schmitt, Irene Sromalski, Blanche Sharkey, Inez Helbing, Lora Gilhart, Elda Follansbee, Esther Koch, and Clara Grieger. They planned the event from how the room would be laid out to the entertainment.

Monthly potlucks on Sunday were discontinued due to the weekend closing of the Center by the City Park and Recreation Committee. However, the potluck dinner never truly was retired. Mention was made of them in 1992, 1993, 1996, 2001, and 2002. Two potlucks were held to celebrate the 40th Anniversary celebration events in 2009 and 2010. The first celebrated the potluck dinner and strawberry feast in June of 2009. The second celebrated a Gold Medal potluck when the Senior Olympics was remembered and the celebration of the winners was held in April of 2010. An event that brought people together to dedicate their time to fun and conversation is too good of an event to ever retire.

The Recreation Band

People were always dedicated to music at the Center from its inception. Such was the case of the Recreation Band under the direction of Ruby Stoltz. This band formed in 1984. They practiced on Monday morning. The band played principally at the Center for recreation and fun.

As dedicated individuals worked toward a purpose, the leadership at the Center and at the City Park and Recreation Department instituted changes that honored individuals, made changes that affected individuals, and changed the way the Center looked and operated.

Updates to the Senior Center in the Dedicated Years

Leisure News—Newsletter Name Change—1990

The Advisory Board asked the question, "Should we change the name of the newsletter?" In 1990, a contest was held and seniors at the Center could vote for the name of the newsletter. Those names in contention were Beaver Tales, Sunburst News, and Leisure News. The votes were tallied as follows: Leisure News 21 votes, Beaver Tales 19 votes, Sunburst News 8 votes. Starting in June of 1990, the newsletter was called Leisure News.

Volunteer of the Month

Articles were placed in the Leisure News honoring volunteers at the Center beginning in 1986. The articles described the history of the volunteer's activities at the Center. Individuals, committees, and groups were honored. The Center's history does not reveal who chose the volunteers. However, it seems as though Director,

Ann Neumaier, did so because the recognition ceased in the newsletter upon her resignation.

Meal Site Anniversary

The 10-year anniversary of the Dodge County elderly nutrition site was celebrated in October 1987. A special meal was prepared and seniors that were at the Center when the meal site opened in 1977 were invited to attend.

Those in attendance were Linda Gunther; Elda Follansbee; Rosa Kohn; Theresa Mack; Sandra Krause, alderperson and chair of the City Parks and Recreation Department; Viola Lohr; Vernetta Horne, Pat Zipeay, coordinator Commission on Aging; Walter Griesbach, Myra Kaiser, benefit specialist for the Commission on Aging; Warren Poland, City Parks and Recreation Director; Inez Helbing, Edwin Karl, Mary Ellen Heck, and Stephanie Levenhagen, nutrition manager for the Commission on Aging.

Advisory Board Changes 1980-1990

1. First Bylaws: The first bylaws were written by the Advisory Committee in 1982, and they were approved by the general membership.
2. Yearly elections for officers began in 1980.
3. Warren Poland, Parks and Recreation Director started coming to the Advisory Board meetings in 1988.
4. The first Treasurer was appointed in 1989. Josephine Rake accepted the position.
5. A manual for volunteer and Advisory Board positions was instituted in 1990.
6. The treasurer was elected by the membership for the first time in 1990.
7. Standing Committees for the Advisory Board were formed in 1990. Woodworking, Tour, Greenhouse, Sunshine, and Membership. Chairs were: Stan Draheim, Woodworking; Mary King, Tour; Wally Griesbach, Greenhouse; Mary Beers, Sunshine; Arline Ledworowski, Membership.
8. A Community Member at Large was appointed to the Board in 1990, Carol Krenz from Bank One accepted the position.
9. A Park and Recreation representative joined the Board in 1990. Cora Moyland accepted this position.

Evening Openings at the Senior Center—1988

In an effort to accommodate the seniors of the community to partake in Senior Center programs, the Senior Center was open one evening a month. This started in 1988. However, it was not successful and the program dissolved in June of 1989.

Park and Recreation Committee Sets Senior Center Rules

The following rules were set down by the Park and Recreation Department in January 1990:

1. <u>No gambling.</u> The City Park and Recreation Department established the policy that no money could be on the tables for the purpose of gambling of any kind at the Center. No games of chance can be played for money on Center premises (euchre, sheep head, bingo).
2. <u>Center Hours.</u> The City Park and Recreation Department established that the Center would not be open on weekends or other City holidays.
3. <u>Sales Tax.</u> The City Park and Recreation Department established that sales tax would have to be charged on all birdhouses, plants, and other items sold from the display case.
4. <u>No Smoking.</u> The City Park and Recreation Department established a "No Smoking" policy for the Center or any rooms with the Center.
5. <u>Rental Policy of the Center,</u> A rental agreement needed to be obtained from the City Park and Recreation Department for persons wishing to rent the Center for events. A Center supervisor was needed on the premises during the rental times. The building was not available for rental on the weekends. The building was not available for rental when Center activities were being held. This policy was enacted in August 1990.

Registration Book/File of Members

A registration book began in 1979 to record who attended the Center. A file of Senior Center members was formulated in 1984.

Center Reference Manual—1989

A Center Reference Manual was published for the first time in 1989. It contained the history, purpose, goals, philosophy of the Center, definition of a multi-purpose Center, Center and trip policies, the job description for volunteers, the bowling league bylaws, and the Center bylaws.

First Memberships in Professional Organizations

The leadership at the Senior Center remained dedicated to issues and challenges facing the senior citizen. That leadership role included joining two organizations that advocated for the senior citizen.

Wisconsin Association of Senior Centers

The Senior Center joined the Wisconsin Association of Senior Centers in September of 1988. The membership was first mentioned in the <u>Leisure News</u> newsletter that year.

Members from the Senior Center attended the conference in April 1992 to gain information at the accreditation session. Cora Moylan drove Good Time Charlie. Those that went were Anne Gartland, Marge Kopff, and Marion Radtke.

Coalition on Aging

Members of the Senior Center attended a meeting at the Wisconsin State Capitol in 1980. The Senior Center joined the Coalition in March of 1981. Our first representatives for that group were Byron and Rita Spangler. The Coalition's major objective was concern for the elderly citizen.

Al Tucker became an alternate representative to the Governing Board in 1992. He attended the Coalition on Aging meetings and reported back to the Steering Committee. Renewal of the membership cost $25 per year.

Remodeling the Senior Center in the Dedicated Years

Dedication to improving the appearance of the Senior Center was ongoing. Improvements were completed by volunteers and contractors and made the Center more energy efficient or improved programming.

1. 1980: A new utility sink and cabinet were placed in the Arts and Crafts room. The floor in that room was painted by Wally Griesbach and Orville Wendt.
2. 1981: The air conditioner was replaced. The Labor Temple donated $50. Wisconsin Electric and the City of Beaver Dam shared the costs of the replacement. The pool table was recovered.
3. 1982: New carpeting and a black and white television were purchased.
4. 1984: An energy savings renovation was completed. The front room windows were removed and replaced with smaller energy efficient windows. New door enclosures and the interior paneling were replaced. The total cost of the project was $17,000. Federal funds were granted for the renovation. Vi Schneider, the Mayor of Beaver Dam, initiated the project.
5. 1985: Air conditioning was placed in the back room.
6. 1987: A shade for the parking lot door (East entry) was purchased.
7. 1989: A vestibule addition was placed in the front of the building (Third Street entry).
8. 1990: The heating system was improved.

Grand Reopening in 1984

A grand reopening occurred on November 13, 1984. The energy efficient remodeling was spotlighted. A professor from UW-Wisconsin spoke and former Mayor Vi Schneider and Mayor John Omen were present.

Handicapped Parking

Handicapped parking spaces were constructed in the parking lot in 1989. This greatly helped those with disabilities who had not had those parking spaces previously.

Wisconsin Conservation Corps Assisted in Senior Center Remodeling in 1988

The Conservation Corps completed improvements to the Center in 1988. The Center was not charged for labor. The Corps volunteers placed <u>insulation</u> above the front room, put energy saving light bulbs in the back room, kitchen, and office areas, and installed <u>new ballasts</u>. The Conservation Corps were a group of young men who worked to improve Wisconsin with building and construction.

Fun and Special Events in the Dedicated Years

Much dedication was placed in the Senior Center; however, there was still time for fun and special events.

Coffee Cake/Drop Cookie Bakeoffs

There was still a dedication to baking and seniors from the Center proudly entered coffee cakes and cookies in order to win each event.

Coffee cake bakeoff winners in November 1990 were: First Place: Gertrude Giese; Second Place: Dorothy Poetter; Third Place: Marion Gade.

Drop Cookie Bakeoff winners in February 1990 were: First Place: Mary Beers; Second Place: Catherine Meyer; Third Place: Dorothy Poetter. Let's hope they had ice cream, too, as the Center provided free ice cream on the second and fourth Wednesday of the month.

Hats Anyone

Decorative hats seemed to be the thing. Participants were encouraged to "show off" their Easter bonnets in 1988. Small prizes were awarded for the best decorated hat. This was repeated in 1992 when men entered the contest. A Spring Hat contest was conducted in April of 1994. In 1999, men were encouraged to escort the ladies in an Easter bonnet parade. As the pictures show, entrants were innovative.

Emerson Schley, Mabel Schley, Viola Lohr,
Evelyn Macksam, Marilyn Balke, Marion Radtke—1992

Corn Roast

The corn roast began in August of 1989 and continued as an annual event. There was also a summer picnic. Eventually around 1997, only an annual picnic was held.

Wheel of Fortune

The popular television game show, Wheel of Fortune, came to the Center in the form of volunteers who assisted John Kraft from WBEV who hosted the game. The game began in January 1990. The wheel was built by Howard Bentz. The puzzle was placed on the blackboard, and wheel watchers spun for prizes on Wednesday afternoons.

Special Volunteers for Special Programs

There are a special set of volunteers who take a program or event to a successful level by their dedication to the event's success. The event is contingent upon their success in how they handle the day, manage the equipment, setup the room, or preplan the day. The success of the day depends on their talent in doing this.

The Tour Escorts

The success of any tour requires a tour escort(s) who is/are dedicated to managing the tour throughout the day. This includes keeping on time, keeping track of passengers, providing entertainment, helping the bus driver with directions, meeting with hotel managers, restaurant managers, event hosts/hostesses, and a wide array of other situations as the "front man or woman" for the tour participants. They must be able to handle emergencies and share conversations with passengers—all with a smile and a pleasant demeanor. The tour guide must care about the guests on the tour.

Day tours (those that begin and end on one day) and extended tours (two days or longer) have been a fundamental part of the Center since 1970. Tours have been scheduled for almost every state in the Union.

Tours to Other Countries

Tours outside the United States began in 1985 when Senior Center travelers traveled to Canada. Overseas tours have gone to Italy, Switzerland, Costa Rica, China, Ireland, Australia/New Zealand, Austria, England, Scotland and Wales.

Tours Within the United States

Travelers from the Senior Center have signed on for tours to Las Vegas, Washington DC, Black Hills, Nashville, New York City, Philadelphia, Yellowstone, Niagara Falls, the Carolinas, and New Orleans to name a few.

Tour committees have planned the trips and advertised them in the newsletter, in brochures, on the radio, and in the newspaper. A formalized trip policy was printed in February 1988 and is updated frequently.

Longest Running Day Trip

A wide array of performances have been seen at the Fireside in Fort Atkinson—our longest running tour. Tours began there on June 3, 1981, when the travelers saw Carousel. Tours continue to go to performances at the Fireside today.

Tour Escort Volunteers

The first tour escort was Audrey Benike, the Director of the Senior Center. Later tour escorts were Viola Lohr, Marion Radtke, Anne Gartland, Marge Kopff, and Phyllis Cullen. The next group of tours escorts was Coleen Brenton, Bunny Schmidt, Ellie Schoeffel, Melody McGowen, Ron Andrews, Del Schultz, Mary Morgan, and Kay and Terry Appenfeldt.

The tour escorts of today are Kay Appenfeldt, Bunny Schmidt, Donna Birschbach, Beth Keitzman, and Wayne Schmitz.

Those escorts in the present and those in the past have been contributors to a successful program at the Center for 40 years.

The Meal Site Workers

The meal site workers have dedicated their volunteer hours since the Dodge County Meal Site was opened in 1977. They wash and set the tables, serve the food, register the people who eat, keep records and clean up the kitchen. The meal site managers oversee the workers. The nutrition program manager is Stephanie Levenhagen and meal site managers have been Marlene Tesch and currently Rose Newman.

Those who assisted as meal site workers are Myrtle Schwantes, Evelyn Beske, Florence Heuer, Florence Hussli, Loraine Ackley, Florence Anderegg, Norma Reiman, Lucille Burbach, Darlene Hein, Marion Radtke, Bill Christian, Arlene (Silloway) Christian, Annie Nielsen, Colleen Hein, Bud and Arline Immerfall, Sharon Kane, Sandy Skalitzky, Audrey Roberts, Vivian Penoske, Beth Ingram, Mary Morgan, and Barb Aplin.

Your assistance has provided many a meal for those who wanted a warm meal, who wanted to be with someone and not alone, and who wanted an hour of conversation and friendship.

B6, I21, N43, G55, O70—Bingo

Without a dedicated bingo caller, how could we play bingo. Bingo has ranked with cards as the most popular game choice at the Center since 1970.

Bingo has been played twice a month, for special events, and weekly at the Center. Bingo prizes have been plants, harvested vegetables and fruits, poultry, seed packets, pennies, and donated prizes.

For the 40th Anniversary celebration in February 2010, penny bingo was played as a remembrance of the past. Wayne Schmitz was the bingo caller and Gert Miller and Charlene Kikkert assisted with prizes.

Bingo volunteers have been Theresa Mack, Irene Udell, Sylvia Frank, Orv Gutgesell, Ida Grant, Geraldine Keel, Marion Radtke, Bill Christian, Gert Miller, Rita Spangler, Bill Thomas, Sid Simonson, Bill Hollihan, Frances Alderden, Kate Pahl, Vivian Penoske, Arline Immerfall, Carol Alexander, Rosemary Godsell, Colleen Hein, Gen Gilmore, Bob Bradley, Loraine Ackley, Annie Nielsen, Del Schultz, Alyce Klarkowski, Charlene Kikkert, Jean Wellbeloved, Kenneth Kroneman, Rena Hughes, Wayne Schmitz, Len Klawitter, and Gladys Wild.

The tables are full for a great day of Bingo

Electronic Bingo System and Bingo Cards

The electronic bingo system was purchased in October 2003. Balls printed with the bingo numbers mechanically rise to the slot. The caller retrieves them from the slot and calls the number. The called numbers are displayed on a lighted screen. How did they do this in days of old?

A set of 100 bingo cards were purchased in November of 1998 for $173.80. They have the plastic slots and players use them today.

Shuffle the Deck and Deal

Dedicated card players have been shuffling the deck, dealing, trumping, selecting blinds, and studying the way they play through euchre, sheep head, pinochle, bridge, and cribbage since the early days of the Center's existence.

For many, cards are an activity that was learned as a child and many come to enjoy a game they learned from little on. Ann Neumaier, Director said, "We have the idea that anybody can play, no matter what their ability."

Playing cards. I'll lead, who has the trump?

Mabel Schley taught sheep head for a multitude of years and served as the volunteer coordinator for the sheep head group for as many years. Current leaders are Diane Neff and Norine Kerecman.

Those who have taught others to play euchre or served as a volunteer coordinator are Marge Kopff, Helen Rannum, Pearl Wollin, Elnora Schkirke, Dorothy Poetter, Lorraine Dittenberger, Marv Gerdes, and Sid Simonson. Del Schultz and Earl Schultz currently teach others how to play euchre and sheep head.

Volunteer coordinators prepare the tables in the room, give out prizes, prepare scorecards, and clean up the room afterwards. Their efforts help those in attendance enjoy the game of cards to pass an afternoon or evening of time.

Public Card Parties

Card playing was extended to the public when the Park and Recreation Department gave permission to have public card parties starting in March of 1999. Nonresident fees were waived. The first public card party was on the third Saturday in May in 1999. The fee to play was $2 which covered lunch and prize money. Euchre was played and Kaye Janisch from the Senior Center Steering Committee organized the event.

Food Preparation for Public Card Parties

For years, Jean Schweisthal voluntarily prepared the lunch at the euchre and sheep head public card parties each month. She purchased the food, kept the costs within budget, cooked the meals, served the meals, cleaned the kitchen, and still enjoyed a game of cards.

Jean Schweisthal and perfect Sheep head score March 27, 2007

Sheep head and the Beaver Dam Conservation Club

The Beaver Dam Conservation Club held a sheep head tournament weekly at the Club in the winter months. The tournament ended in the summer at the Club. Del Schultz contacted the Club to see if the Center could continue the tournament at the Beaver Dam Senior Center in the summer. They agreed and the Center sponsors the tournament from May to November. This started in 2006. The sheep head players fill the room, and the Center has created a partnership with another community organization.

The Bowling League Officers and Secretary

Dedicated co-ed teams hit the alleys each fall until early spring. This has continued since 1974.

A group of bowlers met in August of 1977 to establish the rules and bylaws for the bowling league. Officers were elected to oversee the bowling league.
The officers are President, Vice President, Secretary, and Treasurer. The bulk of the work falls on the league secretary who keeps scores and averages for each bowler, finds subs, and plans holiday events.

An organizational meeting is conducted each fall by the officers of the league where the bylaws are reviewed and schedules are distributed. The dedication of the league officers especially the secretary contributes to the league's functioning effectively during the bowling season.

Presidents who have served are Alvin Schultz, Ed Raschka, June Paul, Evie Lee, Doris Hubatch, Pearl Wollin, Orval Gutgesell, Helen Gloudemann, Marge Kopff, Char Hussli, Joe Quella, LeRoy Fields, and currently Bob Messer.

Vice Presidents who have volunteered are Wally Griesbach, Joanne Bruckman, Pearl Landmann, Marge Kopff, and currently Jenine Bowie.

Treasurers who have served are Frieda Anton and Hester Ruehl who served for lengthy amounts of time. Currently Carol Abel serves as Treasurer.

Secretaries who have served are Esther Hartl, Esther Anderson, Lorraine Krueger, Ed Raschka and currently Betty Eilbes who has served since 1997.

Technology Arrives for Bowling

Bowling software was loaded on the Center computer in 1997. It was purchased by the Senior Center. The software houses the names of the bowlers, compiles the weekly scores and averages, and prepares a tally sheet for each team weekly. Betty Eilbes was the first secretary who used this software; and of course, the software does not work by itself. Betty has to enter the data each week.

Betty Eilbes entering the weekly scores of the bowling league

The Bowling Banquet

The first bowling banquet was April 26, 1984. Trophies were awarded to the first place team. Many of those trophies were brought to the Center and were put on display in the trophy case.

The bowling league was honored as a part of the 40th Anniversary of the Center in September of 2009. Cake and ice cream was served. Prizes were given for the bowler who bowled a 40 in the first game in the 4th frame, for the bowler who bowled a 140 game, for the bowler who bowled a 240 game, and for the bowler who bowled a 440 series—a cute way to honor the 40th anniversary.

Pictures were taken of each team on that September day, and they are proudly displayed at the Senior Center.

With Cue Stick in Hand

Dedicated pool players with cue stick in hand have tried to master the game of pool since the early days of the Center. Friendly competition with one another existed until the opportunity to compete with another Senior Center came into existence in 1984.

Pool League with Waupun Senior Center

The league began in 1984. The teams traveled back and forth between the two centers for weekly games. Wins and losses were tallied. We have the wins and losses for only selected years in our history. For years 1985, 1986, 1988, 1991, 1996, 1997, 1999, 2000, and 2002, Beaver Dam had 480 wins; Waupun had 410 wins. Members of the teams included Del Denzer, Ed Raschka, Jack Schmidt, Rich Krahenbuhl, Don Kopff, Bud Immerfall, Glen Yagodinski, Orval Gutgesell, Max Niggemeier, Merlin Kohl, Chuck Boelter, Bill Milarch, Dan Urban, Les Thiede, Rollie Schweisthal, Chuck Yagodinski, Marv Klawitter, Bill Christian, John Polchinski, Frank Kasper, Wally Griesbach, and Harry Wisniewski.

The league continued every year until 2007 when it was retired due to lack of members to participate—it would not be surprising if the league revived itself again one of these days as the pool players of today continue to "rack them up" weekly at the Center.

The pool league: Standing (left to right) Wayne Gibbs, Terry Appenfeldt, Chuck Yagodinski, Judy Hill, Kay Appenfeldt, Mary Morgan, Len Klawitter, Marsha Horne, Robert Horne. Sitting (left to right) Harvey Schoeffel, Marv Klawitter Not pictured Arden (Bud) Fritz, Lyle Jaehnke

Women Join Pool

Women joined pool in their own league in 1992 with their own time slot on Friday morning. As competition strengthened, women put together a singles pool tournament in 1993 and a doubles pool tournament in 1993 and 1994.

Winners in the 1993 singles tournament were 1) Frieda Anton; 2) Mabel Schley; 3) Marion Radtke. Winners in the 1993 doubles tournament were 1) Loraine Ackley and Frieda Anton; 2) Doris Schumacher and Ann Neumaier; 3) Viola Lohr and Josephine Rake. Winners in 1994 double tournament were 1) Mabel Schley and Geraldine Keel/Doris Schumacher; 2) Loraine Ackley and Marion Radtke.

Mildred Krause and Linda Greeler practicing for Women's Pool League

Men's Pool Tournament

The men began their tournament in 1992 with a singles tournament. Winners were 1) Don Kopff; 2) John Polchinski; 3) Frank Kasper. A men's double elimination event in 1994 had these winners: 1) Del Denzer and Wally Griesbach (who was aged 93); 2) Jim Ackley and Orval Gutgesell.

The Pool Players: Row 1 Wally Griesbach, Harry Wisniewski, John Polchinski, Frank Kasper. Row 2 Bob Spring, Bud Immerfall, Don Kopff, Del Denzer

Now the fun began as it was decided that men and women would compete together.

Co-ed Pool Tournament

Men and women chose partners for this pool tournament in 1994. Winners were 1) Mabel Schley and Merlin Kohl; 2) Mildred Krause and Don Kopff; 3) Frieda Anton and Glen Yagodinski.

Pool Room and Woodshop Change Rooms

In 1991, the pool room and woodshop exchanged rooms—that is the same configuration you see today. In that same year, the pool room and arts and crafts room were lengthened by removing a closet in order to accommodate two pool tables in the pool room.

Pool Room Equipment

Pool cues were bought for the pool room in 1978 and again in 1993. The pool lights mounted over the pool tables were bought in 1993 for $400. The pool tables were recovered in 1997 and again in 2008. Six stools were purchased for the pool room in 1999. They replaced the bench which was then placed by the entry door from the parking lot. It is now in storage.

Two <u>new pool tables</u> were purchased in March of 2000. The former pool tables were donated to the Rock Tavern and the Columbus Senior Center.

<u>Summary of the Dedicated Years</u>

The dedication of the tour guides, bingo coordinators, card coordinators, pool players, and the meal site workers have kept the longest running programs at the Center viable to those attending. Therefore, they deserve to be in this section called the Dedicated Years.

The dedication of the volunteers in this section is to be commended. How lucky we were that they dedicated their time to make the Center a better place which in turn gave the Center a respected reputation in the community. We now move to the Giving Years—the years that our Senior Community extended themselves to the Beaver Dam Community and their own Senior Community by the gifts they gave to them.

SPECIAL STORIES FROM
THE DEDICATED YEARS

Decaffeinated Coffee Anyone. Coffee drinkers were only offered decaffeinated coffee starting in January 1985. Why—for health reasons. The history does not state how well that went over with the coffee drinkers or how long it continued.

Greenhouse Sunday. Wally Griesbach and Marion Radtke would exchange alternate Sundays to sell plants in the greenhouse. This gave both of them a chance to go to church on alternate Sundays.

White Elephants. Volunteers brought rummage items to the Center for a White Elephant sale in conjunction with Ridiculous Days in downtown Beaver Dam. A sale was put together by Ruth Heilman and Byron and Rita Spangler. They sold baked items, popcorn, soda, snow cones, lemonade, and white elephant items. The sale made $300. The proceeds went to charity—$150 to PAVE and $150 to Big Brothers and Sisters.

Noon Hour Wellness. The Parks and Recreation Department offered a free recreational hour at Crystal Lake Beach during the noon hour in 1986. Seniors could walk a 2-mile trail and have a free swim at the beach.

Bluebirds. Don and Marge Kopff donated a print to the Center called "Bluebirds" by artist Terrill Knaack. It is prominently displayed on the wall by the kitchen.

Pooling Around. Jim Ackley was the perfect instructor for the women's pool league—his patience and knowledge were to be commended.

Wally's Game. Wally Griesbach bowled a league game of 243 when he was 91 years old.

A Cleaning Nightmare. The City workers repetitively cleaned the large windows at the Center prior to their being remodeled. It seemed like they were there every other day so they placed metal panels over the top portion of the windows to trim the cost of washing the windows so often.

A Congested Lot. Due to congestion in the Center parking lot in 1990, a volunteer was requested to park cars on trip days.

A Congested Upstairs. Seniors remember when the entire upstairs was filled with birdhouses ready to be shipped to customers.

<u>Croquet Malfunctions.</u> Marion Radtke remembers when her brother, Christian Schultz, would always hit the croquet balls into the water at Tahoe Park. Too bad they didn't have a retriever.

<u>Elmer and June Childress.</u> Elmer and June Childress, television personalities from WMTV Channel 15 in Madison, entertained the Center members in 1990. The cost of the performance was $200 and was sponsored by Walkers ($100) and Jennifers ($100). The event was followed by a potluck dinner.

<u>The Pool Sharks.</u> Mabel Schley said she had an advantage in winning the co-ed pool tournament with Merlin Kohl—she had a pool table at home and practiced with her sons. The other pool players called Merlin and Mabel the "pool sharks" when they walked into the pool room.

<u>The Hat Story Tellers.</u> For Hat Day in 1992, the contestants had to wear a hat and then tell a story about the hat. Mabel Schley won the contest that day by telling a story about her hat and Hawaii. Her hat could conform into many different shapes and she had a story for each shape of the hat.

<u>Hollywood Christmas Show.</u> Volunteers and Advisory Board members from the Center dressed up as Hollywood personalities to entertain Center guests for the annual Christmas skit. All laughed uncontrollably as the volunteers lip synced as the following entertainers: Marion Radtke, Kate Smith; Wally Griesbach, Elvis Presley, Dean Martin, and Bing Crosby; Geri Roedl, Peggy Lee; and Viola Lohr pretended to play like Liberace. Frieda Anton and Sylvia Frank showed their stuff as background dancers. A videotape of the performance can be found in the Center archives.

<u>Clowning Around.</u> The Advisory Board dressed up as clowns for their annual Christmas skit. No one recognized them and everyone was saying "Who are they?"

Frieda Anton said, "That's you Ann Gartland or is it Marion Radtke?"

ANN NEUMAIER
1983-1995

Ann joined the Beaver Dam Senior Center as Director in March of 1983. Ann was a recent graduate of the University of Wisconsin—LaCrosse with a Bachelor's Degree in Recreation and Parks Leadership. She had an extensive background in volunteer services.

Ann was a native of Sauk City and had worked with senior citizens in Monroe as field work to complete her degree. She served as a Girl Scout Leader while in college.

Under her directorship, the Bluebird Restoration project was initiated, the bluebird trails were developed, and thousands of bluebird houses were built and sold nationwide. The woodshop expanded to build a variety of other projects.

The greenhouse was refurbished and renamed the Norm Reier greenhouse. The monthly newsletter was published with colored, heavier paper and advertising was sold for the first time. The first computer was purchased.

Remodeling included reducing the store front window sizes to the size of windows that are there today. New curtains, carpeting, and paneling were installed.

Volunteers actively participated in community events such as the Beaver Dam Sesquicentennial, Beaver Fest, and Senior Olympics. Ann coordinated a strong core of volunteers to assist with Center programs and Center activities. Ann was known to have her Advisory Board put on a Christmas skit each year.

Ann served as President, Past President, and Secretary of the Wisconsin Association of Senior Centers.

Ann said, "My position at the Beaver Dam Senior Center was the most fun position I have held. My job at the Center was like going to a wedding reception every day."

THE GIVING YEARS
1991-2003

The Center members have a generous spirit of giving to the community, to fellow members, and to organizations that help others. Giving includes monetary donations, a helping hand when one is needed, the friendship of music, honoring the nation's veterans and country, sharing of intergenerational thoughts and ideas, building new programs or activities to share with others, or volunteering time at the Center. Such begins the Giving Years and the people who made that possible.

The Christmas Cars

The Christmas cars have become a tradition at the Senior Center. Each year Santa's elves (Senior Center volunteers) hand out cars to children along the Beaver Dam Christmas parade route as a Christmas gift from the Senior Center. They were first handed out at the Christmas parade in 2002. In 2003, elves Evonne Koeppen, Bill Hollihan, and Bill Thomas handed out 600 cars. The amount distributed each year varies, but the sentiment is always there—to put a smile on a child's face at Christmas.

Santa's elves—2009 Back row (left to right) Larry Koeppen, Jack Ulrich, Terry and Kay Appenfeldt (Middle Row) (left to right) Wayne Schmitz, Mary Morgan, Donna Fuhrman, Shirley Mack, Rena Hughes (Front Row) Evonne Koeppen, her daughter Laura and her grandchildren Jack and Jenna.

Elves in previous years were Alice Engebretson, Bill Hollihan, Bill Thomas, Darlene (Butter) Morrissey, Lewis Terlisner, Barb Klossner, John and Marge Haider, Harvey and Ellie Schoeffel, and Don Jacob

It started as an idea formulated by Norma Krahenbuhl. Norma and Rich Krahenbuhl managed the woodshop starting in 1995. Norma went to the Library and researched toy car patterns. When the pattern was found, Rich and the woodshop guys made the cars out of donated wood (2 x 4s). Initially, they were part of the Toy Project. In 2001, 50 bags of toy cars were in storage upstairs at the Center. They were distributed to area children at Christmas and the Christmas cars were born.

Each year a new pattern is used and a new set of cars are ready by early December. Senior Center volunteers cut out each car, sand them, put on wheels, and dip them in tung oil for preservation. Each car is branded with the Senior Center logo. The elves have been told that some children have collected them all and look forward to adding to their collection each year.

A history of Christmas cars—2001-2010

The Toy Project

Donating toys to ill children—what a great idea. Rich Krahenbuhl, woodshop manager, conceived the idea to craft toys for children in February 2000. Ed Raschka made the first prototype for a set of blocks. Mitsy Raschka made the fabric bag to hold them. Amy Palm, Director, said, "It's a way to give back to the community."

The primary purpose was to give the bagged toys to ill children at Beaver Dam Community Hospital. The gift bags were made by Center members—some sewing them at their homes. All bags were made out of donated fabric.

The toys were made from donated wood (2 x 4s) by the woodshop guys. The toy block sets sold for $3, the wooden cars for $3, and both together sold for $5 for those who wished to purchase them.

Left to right: Ed Raschka, Mitzy Raschka, Gail Hope Henschel, BDCH, Norma Krahenbuhl, Rich Krahenbuhl with the display of toy blocks, toy cars, and bagged toys (Photo Courtesy of Beaver Dam Daily Citizen)

Santasyland—1992

Dave Roedl from Hillendale Parkway on Hwy E in Beaver Dam designed a special land for underprivileged children for Christmas. It included a candy cottage, skating rink, nativity scene, performance stage, lighted trails through the woods, and Santa's house.

Senior Center volunteers made wooden ornaments and wooden mittens to give to the children of Santasyland as Christmas gifts. Those volunteers were Bob Jeske, Del Denzer, Art Wallendal, Eve Hussli, Sylvia Frank, Lorraine Krueger, Viola Lohr, Frieda Anton, Marion Radtke, Dorothy Poetter, Marge Kopff, Beth Ingram, Loraine Ackley, Doris Schumacher, and Anne Gartland. They made and painted 1,000 wooden Christmas ornaments and 1,200 wooden mittens.

Bluebird Trails

Donating bluebird houses to make bluebird trails was the next project conceived by Don Kopff and the bluebird house builders. A bluebird trail consists of 10-15 bluebird houses on fence posts or trees along the edge of a farm field. Volunteers installed the houses about four feet above the ground. Don Kopff and his bluebird trail volunteers would contact local farmers to put up the bluebird trails. Initially, all the bluebird houses were donated by the woodshop at the Senior Center. Woodshop volunteers helped in building the trails. Volunteers were Merlin Domann, Floyd Schreiber, Stan Draheim, John Kaczmarski, Fran Kowalchyk, Joe Molz, Tim Schweiger, Grover Grady, Tim Giese, Harry Wisniewski, Neils Nielson, Henry Kroll, Bob Spring, and Frank Kasper.

Bluebird Trail on Hwy 151

In 1994, the State Department of Transportation gave Don Kopff permission to put 500 to 600 bluebird houses from Beaver Dam to Sun Prairie on Hwy 151. The houses were placed in pairs 12 to 14 feet apart with overall spacing of 100 to 150 yards. This followed BRAW guidelines and allowed distance and territorial rights for the birds. The houses were placed on the west side of the highway. The trail construction began in 1994.

Bluebird house 15 on Hwy 151

Signs Marking the Bluebird Trail

In July 1994, permission was needed from the Township of Beaver Dam, the Department of Transportation, and the commercial business, Neuman Pools to mount the bluebird trail sign on Hwy 15l. Permission was granted and a 4 foot x 8 foot sign was placed along the highway.

A similar sign was placed at Sunset Hills Golf Course in 1993. It marked the bluebird trail around the golf course.

The Bluebird Restoration Sign on Hwy 151

Sites of Bluebird Trails

Besides Hwy 151 and Sunset Hills, bluebird trails were placed at the Wastewater Treatment Plant in Beaver Dam, Old Hickory Golf Course, Crystal Lake Park, St. Peter's and Oakwood Cemeteries, Airport Road and Bayside Park, a farm on Hwy G South, the Trailer Court by Hwy 151 bridge, both sides of 151 to Waupun, Memorial Garden Cemetery, Astico Park, Derge Park, Beaver Dam Rod & Gun Club, Dodge County Fairgrounds, and ProBuild to Cty Rd DE.

In 1997, 45 bluebird houses were donated to Boy Scout Post 3750 to construct a bluebird trail at Crystal Lake Park.

In 1999, fifth graders at Prairie View Elementary School constructed a bluebird trail on the school grounds. Bluebird kits were donated by the Senior Center, and the students put them together. Parents and students set the poles and attached the bird houses. It gave students an opportunity to work with the Senior Center volunteers, an opportunity to learn building skills with their parents, and gave them a mini course focusing on the environment.

Later, starting in 1998, people who wanted a bluebird trail of six or more bluebird houses put on their own property paid for the houses and posts. If they could not build the trail themselves, the Center charged a small fee for the Senior Center volunteers to come to their property and build the trail.

Maintaining the Trail—Bluebird Trail Monitors

Each fall the bluebird houses on the trails are cleaned by a core of volunteers. The old nests are cleaned out, and the entry holes are closed or left open to keep mice out in the winter.

In November 1994, senior center volunteers worked alongside the Grace Presbyterian Church Cub Scouts and Sunday School students to clean the bluebird trail south of the City of Beaver Dam. It was also a learning trip as students were taught how to recognize wren, sparrow, swallow, and bluebird nests which can all inhabit a bluebird house.

Rich Krahenbuhl, Senior Center volunteer shows a student how to nail a bluebird house shut for the winter (Photo Courtesy of Beaver Dam Daily Citizen)

Neal Lofberg currently maintains the bluebird trails at the Cemetery south on Center Street, the County Park past the Marina, the Wastewater Treatment Plant in Beaver Dam, the Beaver Dam Country Club (front and back nine), Old Hickory Golf Course, Crystal Lake Park, St Peter's and Oakwood Cemeteries, Airport Road and Bayside Park, Memorial Garden Cemetery, Derge Park, Beaver Dam Conservations Club, and ProBuild to DE. Bluebird trails have also been monitored by Jack Ulrich, Rip Cullen, church and Boy Scout troops, service organization members, church and Sunday school members, Art Wallendahl, Bob Hanser, Don Kopff, and Jack Bartholmai.

Not only did the bluebird profit from these trails, but any children that volunteered also profited. They profited by learning about suitable nesting conditions for birds, determined types of bird nests, and had the satisfaction of helping the bluebird population—once extinct in Dodge County. The Senior Center volunteers and Don Kopff can be proud of the nests they built, the trails they built, the birds they saved, and the children and populace they educated.

Meals on Wheels

Meals on Wheels began in 1973 for delivering warm meals to homebound individuals. The Senior Center served as a site for meal pickup and delivery. The earliest record for activity at the Center is 1980. Meal site volunteers packaged the meals. Volunteers (many of whom were Senior Center members) came to the Center to pick up the meals, used their own cars, and delivered the meals to designated sites around the City of Beaver Dam. The program stopped at the Senior Center in June 2008 when it became permanently housed at Beaver Dam Community Hospital.

The Gift of Music

The gift of music can be shared with all who wish to hear the sound. The following musicians gave the gift of music to their fellow senior citizen members and to the community. Their talent provided a moment of tranquility, a moment of relaxation, a moment of beautiful sound, or a moment of shared entertainment.

O' Ye Queen's Court Minstrels

This Renaissance and Baroque musical group with Director, Thomas Droegskemp began in 1991. Volunteers from the Center played recorders/harpsichords which were purchased by the Center. They dressed in shawls and chiffon scarves with Elizabethan hats. They entertained various groups on behalf of the Center; however, their gift of music was short lived and they dissolved in 1992. Their instruments were sold to the Oak Park Recorder School.

Ye Queen's Court Minstrels

A Kitchen Band Which Became the Third Street Band

Oscar and Deloris Mellenthin came back from a trip to Arizona with a great idea—let's form a kitchen band like we saw in Arizona. To keep the idea going, they met with Sally Kramer who had a kitchen band called the Brookfield Kitchen Band. From this exploration, they formed a band whose first name was the Elderberries. Oscar was the producer and Rita Spangler was the Director.

Prime Time and the Third Street Band

In September 2003, the Third Street Band was spotlighted in Prime Time a special section of a local newspaper specifically for active adults 50 and better. The Band was interviewed at a restaurant in Waupun. They were asked to perform and gave a performance for the surprised customers in attendance.

The Instruments the Original Third Street Band Played

The Third Street Band gave its premier performance at the Senior Center on June 18, 2003. Band members that day were Lynn Winkie, Oscar Mellenthin, Julian Buss, Gloria Klug, Esther Buss, Rita Spangler, Arline Immerfall, Loraine Ackley, and Deloris Mellenthin.

The kitchen band played the following unique instruments. Rita Spangler, Stumpf fiddle; Marion Radtke, sand blocks; Esther Buss, keyboard; Loraine Ackley, tambourine; Deloris Mellenthin, washboard; Audrey Bartell, ratchet sand blocks;

Lester Wiersma, horn; Barb Hunt, kazoo; Gloria Klug, triangle. Other band members included were Julian Buss, Marilyn Neuman, Lynn Winkie, and Arline Immerfall

In 2002, Bob Zomora designed a logo to match the new name of the band—the Third Street Band. This logo is displayed every time the band performs.

Third Street Band Logo designed by Bob Zomora

Rita Spangler and the Stumpf fiddle

Rita is a Stumpf fiddle player extraordinaire. The Stumpf fiddle is a walking stick with a bell, horn, woodblock, springs, and tin pan drum attached.

Rita got her Stumpf fiddle from her husband, Byron, as a gift. She said, "I can't play this thing." He said, "Let's take lessons from Cele." This led to a career for Rita who played with the Mellow Tones, Harvey Ansay's band. She continues to play the Stumpf fiddle with the Third Street Band.

The Band started as a Kitchen Band and then broadened their performances to a singing and vaudeville troupe. Rita Spangler was instrumental in creating skits and performances for both bands. Rita also serves as the keeper of the history of the Band.

Third Street Band Members (left to right) Gloria Klug,
Esther Buss, and Rita Spangler and the Stumpf fiddle

"Musical Ambassadors" for the Beaver Dam Senior Center

The Third Street Band is labeled as "Musical Ambassadors" because of the diversity of entertainment they provide as a singing and vaudeville troupe. As a group they travel to locations in Beaver Dam and surrounding communities in order to perform. All of the performers donate their time. They average 41 performances a year at an average age of 75.

Places they have performed are at senior centers, nursing homes, the Senior Expo, churches, concerts in the Park, festivals, holiday events, birthdays, reunions, block parties, and parades.

Some past and present members of the Band as of the 40th Anniversary are Director Rita Spangler, Irene Bell, Bev Grams, Bob Bradley, Marilyn Neuman, Audrey Bartell, Bev Carlson, Barb Hunt, Ron Andrews, Rena Hughes, Dot Schultz, Marty Megale, Elaine Koehn, Diane Kalmes, Ron Gagnon, Mary Desjarlais, and Peg Slez, Keyboard and Musical Director.

Peg Slez currently coordinates song and costume choices, provides the lead in to the songs as keyboard player, coordinates the activities done on the day of the performance, and introduces the performers.

As Rita Spangler says, "I perform to make someone feel good and if you sing, you pray twice."

Third Street Band. Front Row (left to right) Irene Bell, Audrey Bartell, Rita Spangler, Mayor Tom Kennedy, Elaine Koehn, Marty Megale. Back row (left to right) Peg Slez, Barb Hunt, Bev Carlson, Diane Kalmes, Dot Schultz, Mary Desjarlais Not in picture: Bob Bradley, Rena Hughes, Wayne Schmitz

The Juke Box That Played by Itself

Remember the juke box in the game room that would mysteriously just start playing a song. You never knew what song it would play from a Frank Sinatra hit to a Big Band tune. It was like it wanted to share its gift of music for all to enjoy.

The juke box was purchased from Modern Specialties in Madison for $500. The purchase was made in December of 1994. It held 100 records.

The previous paragraphs have shared the gift of giving for the community. The following paragraphs share the gift of giving for the Senior Center community. Here is that story.

The Sunshine Program

Generous women have taken their personal time to select greeting cards, to send those cards, and sometimes to visit those who are ill or in need of comfort after the death of a loved one. Sunshine chairs have included Elda Follansbee, Mary Beers, Sylvia Frank, Anne Gartland, Geraldine Keel, Doris Schumacher, and Arline Ledworoski. Currently Mabel Schley serves as the volunteer coordinator and has done so for fifteen or sixteen years. Mabel always includes a personal note in her own handwriting to hopefully uplift the spirits of the person receiving the card.

Cash Memorials from the Advisory Board

The Advisory Board in June 1998 voted to give a cash memorial of $25 to the spouse or family of a deceased Center volunteer, president or past member of the Steering Committee. The money was taken from the project account. However, it became hard to find or recognize the deceased members so the project was stopped in April 1999.

Tree of Lights

The Advisory Board gave a monetary donation from the project account to the Tree of Lights program at Beaver Dam Community Hospital. They purchased three lights in 1990—one for deceased Senior Center members, one for current living Senior Center members, and one honoring Senior Center volunteers. Donations continued in 1993 and 1994 as a remembrance for those who passed away, the hospice program, and Lifeline. The donations continued through 2001.

The Gift of Giving—Christmas Gifts from Mabel Schley

How do you recognize a good heart—a caring heart. Mabel Schley has been donating Christmas gifts to Senior Center members for 19 years.

Originally, Christmas gifts were donated by local merchants. Senior Center volunteers would go to local merchants and ask for donations to be used as Christmas gifts. "It felt like begging," said Mabel.

So Mabel went to the Director of the Senior Center and asked to discontinue asking merchants for gifts. "I'll furnish the gifts instead," said Mabel.

Mabel says, "I enjoy seeing people get a gift." It is Mabel's way to help the Center. Mabel would buy the gifts all year long and store them in a large room in her home. Come Christmas, she and her son would bring the gifts to the Center where they were wrapped and given away at the Christmas party. For Christmas 2007, Mabel purchased 67 gifts—her highest amount.

A good heart—a caring heart. That's Mabel.

Mabel Schley

Volunteer Breakfast

Every year the Center has remained a viable and progressive Center due to a core of volunteers who give their time to teach classes, to manage events, to think of new ideas and programs, to chair committees and meetings, to supervise the Center at parties, to serve as volunteer coordinators for programs and activities, to work in the office, to create and build projects, to decorate the Center for holidays, to serve meals and setup the meal site, to serve on the Steering Committee, and a multitude of other services.

The first volunteer breakfast was held in 1986 at Hotel Rogers. It honored the volunteers who gave their time in van driving, being a hostess, serving on the tour committee, serving on the advisory board, working in the greenhouse, the sunshine person, the bingo and euchre coordinators, and the bowling league officers.

In the '90s, separate volunteer breakfasts were held for the greenhouse and the woodshop as well a separate breakfast for all volunteers.

Volunteer Logs

In 2002, volunteer logs were implemented and members logged in and entered their volunteer hours. This gave the Center the ability to track volunteer hours. The totality of hours ranged from 7,000 to 9,000 hours of volunteer time in a year.
Volunteers directly benefit the Center by assisting with programs and activities. The satisfaction of contributing to the Center is a benefit to the volunteer also. All that can be said is that through their efforts nearly 100 programs are offered at the Center in Senior Center and Recreation activities.

The Directors have sought different ways to honor the volunteers—the volunteer breakfast seems to be the most popular. It will always be there to be used by a Director to recognize the time and talent provided by a given year's core of volunteers.

Volunteer Breakfast Volunteers—2004

Sometimes a talented individual is willing to share their knowledge with others—to teach a skill that others may enjoy. The next section recognizes those individuals who shared their skills with the senior population who signed on for their classes at the Center.

Crocheting with Marion Gade

Marion Gade taught her first classes in Beginning and Advanced Crocheting in 1977. Marion continues to teach today which encompasses 33 years of providing instruction at the Center. Marion also teaches rug braiding. Her classes share conversation and patterns, crochet for worthwhile causes, and make projects for their individual use.

The efforts of Marion and her classes have been magnanimous to our community, to other communities, and overseas. Here are three projects that have really made a difference.

Project Linus

Marion's crochet students crocheted afghans for Project Linus. Project Linus is a project from the Madison area, and the crocheted afghans are donated to children of all ages who are hospitalized in the Madison area. The wish is that it will keep them warm and comforted during their time of illness. Most of the yarn is donated by people from the community, or Marion goes to rummage sales or second hand shops and finds the yarn. These wonderful ladies have made more than 1000 afghans. Ladies who crocheted afghans are Marion Gade, Sue McMurry, Marie Sears, Colleen Hein, Charlene Litwin, Deb Huebner, Marie Frank, Sue Mlodzik, Dot Hankes, Nina Wiesmueller, Carol Ward, and Bertha Blyme.

Shawls for Nursing Homes

The crochet ladies crocheted shawls and lap robes from donated yarn for nursing home residents in our area. The wide array of designs was created individually by each member. However, Marion provided instructions and patterns.

Ladies involved in this project are Marion Gade, Marie Sears, Sue McMurry, Gerri Roedl, Pat Kuehl, Charlene Litwin, Debbie Huebner, Donna Dye, Dorothy Hankes, Marie Frank, Colleen Hein, and Katherine Seigner.

Seated (left to right) Volunteer Coordinator, Marion Gade; Marie Sears, Sue McMurry, Gerri Roedl. Standing (left to right) Pat Kuehl, Charlene Litwin, Debbie Huebner, Donna Dye, Dorothy Hankes, Marie Frank, Colleen Hein, Katherine Seigner

Caps for the Capitol

The Knitting Class with instructor Martha Bauernfeind and Marion's crochet class collaborated to make infant caps. The caps were sent to the capital in Madison. The caps were shipped overseas to infants in impoverished countries. Those helping from the crochet class were Nina Wiesmueller, Charlene Litwin, Colleen Hein, Marion Gade, Marie Frank, Debbie Huebner, Marie Sears, Sue McMurry, Dot Hankes, and Pat Kuehl.

Knitting Class for Caps for the Capitol
(left to right) Martha Bauernfeind, Janice Holt, Amena Akhter, Darlene Wright

Woodcarving—Oscar Mellenthin

In 1997, a talented individual named Oscar Mellenthin donated his time to teach a woodcarving program at the Senior Center. He started this class when he was 80 years old.

He said the staples of the class were, "a knife, a block of wood, and Band aids." He also said, "Once they get started on this, they'll be hooked." They are still "hooked" carving basswood or walnut into fish, kangaroos, angels, totem poles, bears, Packer players, or anything else. Oscar taught the class two hours per week.

The class continued under the leadership of Don Jacob, who learned the craft from Oscar. When Don passed away, Marsha Horne agreed to be the Volunteer Coordinator for the group.

Woodcarvers from left to right:
Corwin Miller, Paul King, Don Jacob, Oscar Mellenthin

The wood carvers carved the miniature artifacts representing programs on the clock face of the 40th Anniversary clock in 2009. Their craft will forever be a wonderful memory for the history of the Senior Center.

Woodcarvers: (left to right) Duane Schroeder, Louis Antonioni, Eric Huizenga, Lloyd Lathrop, Carolyn Utrie, Alyce Schoenwetter, Marsha Horne. Seated: Dale Schermerhorn, Paul King, Jack Ulrich, Graham Ross, Harold Ninmann, Don Jacob. Not pictured. Gary Moody, Corwin Miller, James Erdmann, Harold Vanderhei

Genealogy—2001

In 2001, Sally Adam offered a genealogy club at the Center. In 2002, Mary Lou Navarrette served as the genealogy coordinator. In 2003, volunteer Lynn Winkie served as the coordinator. The group traces their family tree, finds someone from their family tree, or assists the beginner to get started. Lynn continued with the class through 2004 when he retired.

Sally Adam has been the volunteer coordinator since 2004. A noted Civil War historian, Sally has a wealth of knowledge to offer to the members who have started or have continued with the club. Members will gladly show you their printed family trees and offer lots of assistance whether from the computer or specialized organizations to find your family members. It takes a special kind of research and a talented researcher. It is a special club that does a special task.

Genealogy Club: (left to right) Sally Adam, Genealogy Coordinator; Nancy Jo Falbe, Audrey Roedl, Marianne Miller, Gloria Derge, Martha Strieff, Not pictured Margaret Schmitt Deceased Don Jacob

Exercising with Jane Haldiman

Moraine Park Technical College instructor, Jane Haldiman, led the way with chair exercise and easy workouts to limber the joints and build the muscles of those who attended starting in 1997. Her class continued until 2005. Students enrolled in the co-ed class for 18-week sessions.

The Book Club

The Book Club began in December 2000. Coleen Brenton, Center Office Assistant, helped the Club members by ordering the books and checking them out to members. Lively book discussions continue today on a monthly basis. Patti Maleck, Customer Service for the Senior Center, currently orders the books and coordinates dispensing them to Book Club members.

Book Club Members: (left to right) Front Row. Ruth Elgersma, Mary Ann Hussli, Marilyn Neuman, Ann Maas. Back Row. Colleen Hein, Betty Kuiper, Alyce Klarkowski, Volunteer Coordinator Charlene Kikkert. Not pictured: Shirley Precht, Judy Beyer, Marion Soldner, Marge Ferrell, Marge Haider, Audrey Bartell, Eileen Brower, Shirley Graham, Lorna Schultz.

Computers Arrive

The first computer and printer arrived at the Center in September 1996. A grant from the Learning Foundation of Wisconsin gave computers and printers to Jefferson School, Williams Free Library, and the Senior Center to instruct Internet access.

In 1997 and 1998, the third and fourth graders at Jefferson School met with Senior Center members on Tuesday and Thursday for 45-minute sessions. Students taught computer skills to the seniors—seniors shared their lives and heritage. The classrooms of Teri Dary and Jesse Peters were used.

In 1997, the Beaver Dam Unified School District provided free instruction to seniors on how to write letters and use word processing on a Windows operating system computer. The Beaver Dam High School offered eight computer courses at the Career Center free of charge to seniors in 1998.

In 1999, Level 1 and Level 2 Intermediate Windows 95 were taught to seniors through the Beaver Dam Unified School District at the Middle School. Instructors were Gene DeGroot and Barb Ludtke. "The seniors are eager to learn and willing to practice between classes, " said Barb Ludtke. "They are no longer afraid and see that they can use technology as a senior citizen." One full session was devoted to Internet and E-mail giving seniors the ability to E-mail children and grandchildren. "They want to keep up with the world around them," said Jana Stephens, Senior Center Director. The program continued for three years.

In 1999, the one computer at the Center was available for anyone to use. However, those wanting to use the computer had to sign up ahead of time.

Computer Room at the Senior Center

In 2000, the Steering Committee approved purchasing two computers with a budgeted cost of $1000 each. They also approved opening a computer lab in the Arts and Crafts Room.

In September 2000, the computer lab opened with three computers with software and Internet access. With the other computer already on site, the Computer Lab now had three computers.

Computer Classes Started

In September 2000, computer classes started at the Center. The instructors were Bob Frankenstein, Beginning Computers; and Chuck Stambaugh, Internet.

In January 2001, Bob continued teaching Beginning Computers; and Coleen Brenton began teaching a Word Processing class. In March of 2001, Harvey Schoeffel began teaching an Internet class; and Amy Palm and Linda Janz taught Internet and E-mail.

In 2002, Coleen continued teaching Word Processing; Dennis Levenhagen taught Beginning Computers; and Linda Janz taught Internet and E-mail.

Handicapped Computer Instruction

In 2001, Kathryn Barbour donated a handicapped computer including a monitor, keyboard, mouse, and software to allow handicapped persons to type.

Generations On-line

In 2003, Generations On-Line a computer teaching program for elderly adults helped each learn the Internet. Beginning classes, Internet one-on-one lessons, and word processing classes were offered. Scanners and printers were now available in the computer lab. Specialty classes were available upon request. The computer room was open to anyone to use during Senior Center hours of operation.

All of these teachers whether they volunteered their time, were paid, or taught from Moraine Park Technical College gave of their talent to improve the lives of the senior community at the Senior Center. The gift of education can never be taken away.

Intergenerational—Let's Meet the Children

Youth Baseball League

The Advisory Committee of the Senior Center approved sponsoring a Youth Baseball team in 1994 and 1995. The teams were composed of seven—and eight-year olds.

Brownies and Pioneer Groups

Center volunteers worked with a Brownie Troop in a program called "Hand to Hand Badge" in 1996. Volunteers worked with each girl to help each earn their badge. The Brownies earned their badges by working with a senior volunteer.

The Pioneer group for St. Stephens Lutheran Church arrived in October 1998 for an evening session. Senior volunteers helped them build birdhouses.

Kids Involved Directly with Seniors—1998

The program was developed by teachers and students at Beaver Dam Middle School. The program promoted communication and understanding between the generations. Center volunteers and students built birdhouses, played cards, played pool, or worked together in the greenhouse.

Teaching and playing cards with middle school students

Seconds and Seniors

The program matched Center volunteers with second graders at Lincoln School in a special program called Seconds and Seniors. Seniors read stories and listened to second graders read to them. There was a different theme each week. The program had instructional books which followed a set program each week. Activities pertaining to each theme were completed. They met twice a month for an hour or two. Materials were supplied from a grant awarded to Judy Hein, the second grade instructor. The program continued for three years—1999, 2000, 2001.

Building Bluebird and Wren Kits

In 2003, Jim Schwartz, woodshop manager, and Fritz Wagner used their building skills to create bluebird and wren kits. The houses were divided into sections (nails were included) and packaged with instructions for construction.

The original bluebird kits to make bluebird houses

Volunteers from the woodshop have helped children build those houses every year since the kits were first built. Children from 4H groups, school groups, Cub Scouts, Boy Scouts, the Clover Bud Explorer Day Camp, recreation activities in the park in the summer, and others asked the volunteers from the woodshop to stop by with their kits and help children construct a birdhouse. Jim would travel to several events a year where he sold kits to make a profit for the Senior Center. The shop even has its own set of hammers for the children to use.

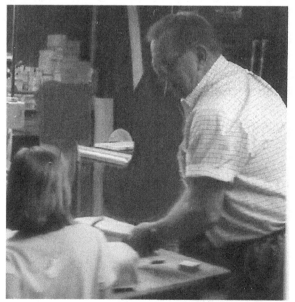

Jim Schwartz and friend building a birdhouse

Honoring Our Veterans

Veterans Quilt Project

A cooperative project occurred between Beaver Dam High School social studies students and thirty veterans who were found at the Beaver Dam Senior Center. It was called the Veterans Quilt Project.

Senior students interviewed veterans. The students created a short story and a quilt block from the veteran's interview. Questions that were asked were: What is your name? Where are you from originally? What years were you in the service? How did you become part of the war—enlisted or drafted? What branch of the service were you in and what was your assignment? Where were you stationed? What was the highest rank you attained? Did you receive any medals, ribbons, or other awards? What was you most memorable experience? What was your proudest moment? How long did you stay in the service? For the quilt block, the student placed the veteran's name and their name somewhere on the block. The blocks were stitched together to make a quilt. Nancy's Notions donated the material for the blocks. Dianne Thompson from Nancy's Notions stitched the quilt and put it in its final form. Jim Schwartz, the Senior Center woodshop manager, made the display hanger.

The veterans who participated were Jim Ackley, Bob Bradley, Bob Frankenstein, Pete Gove, Paul Hoffman, Bud Immerfall, Bob Jeske, Marie Kuenzi, Bill Milarch, Dick Neuman, Burt Prest, Harold Reif, Clifford Schwartz, Fritz Wagner, Cletus Willihnganz, Burt Beyer, Julian Buss, Ken Gohr, Roger Hasbrouck, Bill Hollihan, Don Jacob, Merlin Kohl, Larry Mielke, Leon Neis, John Polchinski, John Rabata, Jack Schmidt, Bud Snow, Carol Wegner, and Lynn Winkie.

Student interviewers were Sam Evans, Sarah Welsch, Lindy Czarneski, Katelynn Strieff, Valerie Syrjamaki, Emily Schultz, Kristi Parker, Katie Lauff, JoDee Nagler, Whitney Stofflet, Allie Wade, Jenny Rezutek, Ben Rohr, Krystle Kurdi, Scott Thompson, Liz Corey, Amy O'Connor, Sarah Schmid, Jenna Haack, Megan Lachowica, Kelley Schulteis, Emily Walton, Natalie Kempf, Jackie Sirota, Sarah Steinbacher, Kristi Scott, Jeni Janz, Charles Allhands, Jessica Link, and Shelly VanBuren.

Hanging the Veterans Quilt

A formal dedication ceremony to honor the veterans and to hang the quilt occurred on November 11, 2003—Veteran's Day. The ceremony was held at the Senior Center. The students and veterans that participated in the project were the honored guests. Cake and beverages were served. The Third Street Band performed. Peter Woreck, lead instructor for this project, and Dianne Thompson, the quilt maker, unveiled the quilt at the ceremony.

The Veteran's Quilt—Peter Woreck Instructor for the Project and
Dianne Thompson, quilt maker

The quilt occupies a wall at the Senior Center. The book of essays that the students wrote occupies a space with the quilt.

The veterans and students donated their time to make a masterpiece—a true remembrance of giving. The veterans gave for their country, and the students gave them a place in history at the Center.

Veterans Memorial Drive

The Beaver Dam Senior Center donated two trees that were planted on Veterans Memorial Drive in Beaver Dam in 1990.

Veterans and Home Front Exhibit at the Dodge County Historical Society—2001

In June, the Steering Committee approved the donation of an oak case to house artifacts for the Veterans and Home Front exhibit at the Dodge County Historical Society. The exhibit was called "Beaver Dam Community Goes to War."

Veterans Program 2002

On Veteran's Day, November 11, 2002, veterans received a free lunch at the Senior Center. A special program was presented by Bob Frankenstein.

Veterans Memorial Bench at Oakwood Cemetery

The Steering Committee of the Beaver Dam Senior Center approved a donation of $2500 for a marble bench at the Veterans Memorial at Oakwood Cemetery. Family members and friends may sit on this bench to reflect and remember their loved ones. The bench reads, "Respectfully Donated by Beaver Dam Senior Center." The monies were taken from the Project Account in August 2003.

Veterans Memorial Bench

It continues to be an honor to recognize the veterans each Veterans Day and Memorial Day with programs or activities devoted to their service to their country.

The text continues with another form of giving. The Beaver Dam Senior Center through the Steering Committee gave monetary donations to charitable organizations and those in need of help. Thus, begins the story of another form of giving.

Monetary Donations Given to the Community

Monetary donations were given to organizations in support of their mission beginning in 1986. Here is a list of those that received donations: Beaver Dam Community Hospital, PAVE, Dodge County Human Services, Foster Children of Dodge County, Camp Wabeek, Easter Seals, Department of Human Services for 48 foster families, Lutheran Social Services, Foster Parents, Open Arms Homeless Shelter, Beaver Dam Police Department for the Bike Patrol Unit, Salvation Army, Big Brothers and Big Sisters, New Beginnings Homeless Shelter, and the WBEV/WXRO Children's Radiothon.

People suffering tragedy also were helped. Those included: Elder to Elder Disaster Relief in Tallahassee, Florida, after a hurricane; Wautoma Senior Citizen Center after a tornado; and flood victims in North Dakota.

Conservation also benefited as donations were given to the Wild Goose Trail Fund, Beaver Dam Lake Restoration, and Beaver Dam Lake Association.

Entertainment for the community was also considered in the monetary donations that were given for Must Skis and for a multitude of Concerts in the Park over several years.

Donating $200 for Beaver Dam Police Department Bike Patrol
(left to right) Jana Stephens, Senior Center Director, Al Tucker, Steering Committee Chairperson; Mary Reilly, Steering Committee Treasurer; Officer Tom Mayer (Photo Courtesy of Beaver Dam Daily Citizen)

The Steering Committee of the Beaver Dam Senior Center donated thousands of dollars for the benefit of others. It seems as though the people of the Senior Center have always been generous from the first days when they had no money and gave money from their own wallets for coffee, door prizes, and food for potlucks. The generosity of their time to countless programs, activities, events, and people is a true measure of a giving senior community which just happens to be housed at the Beaver Dam Senior Center.

Decisions about the Senior Center were ongoing and are reflected in the following paragraphs.

Good Time Charlie is Retired

Good Time Charlie was retired in 1986, and a new van was purchased by the City for Senior Center use. In 1991, two wide-hinged steps with a greet bar were purchased for the van for handicapped seniors. The van was stored in the shed on the Senior Center property.

Taxi Service Began in 1996

The Steering Committee began discussing transportation to and from the Center in 1996. A van usage survey asked questions of Senior Center members in February 1997. The van was retired somewhere between this time and 1998.

The taxi cab service began August 19, 1996. Discounts were provided to senior citizens within the city limits.

Beginning In December 1998, subsidized taxi rides were provided by the City of Beaver Dam for seniors to participate in Senior Center programs and activities.

Phone Number Change

The phone number was changed in August of 1994. The phone number was changed to 920-887-4639.

Steering Committee Replaces the Advisory Board

The Advisory Board was renamed as the Steering Committee in 1996. The Committee consisted of seven members. Five members were to be elected by ballot. Two additional members would be the Park and Recreation representative and the Senior Center Director. Standing Committees were Bowling, Greenhouse, Membership, Community Service, Program, Tour, and Woodshop.

Woodshop Safety Courses—City Insurance Coverage

Everyone working in the woodshop was required to take a shop safety course starting in September 1992. This was required by the City's insurance carrier. A decision by the governance of the City of Beaver Dam determined that volunteers in the woodshop would not be covered by City insurance starting in 2001. A letter reflecting that change and written by the City Attorney is posted in the woodshop. Therefore, the woodshop would go practically unused after that time because volunteers did not want to work when they were not covered by insurance.

AARP Meetings Scheduled at the Senior Center

The Steering Committee approved that AARP could hold meetings at the Senior Center. The meetings were held on the second Thursday of each month starting in

2001. The Steering Committee believed the Center members would benefit from the excellent speakers that AARP provided.

Habitat for Humanity and the Woodshop

The Habitat for Humanity volunteer project requires a volunteer to put in service hours as part of their qualification to join the organization. In 2002, Rich Krahenbuhl worked with a Habitat for Humanity volunteer to complete his service hours in the Senior Center woodshop. Tony made butterfly houses.

Age Requirement for Senior Center Membership is Changed

The age requirement for senior membership at the Senior Center when it opened was 55 years of age. This continued until 2002 when the age requirement was lowered to 50 years of age. That age requirement continues today.

Website Address is Acquired

The City of Beaver Dam website was created in December of 2003. A web page was provided for the Senior Center. The web address is www.cityofbeaverdam.com

Voting at the Center

The Center serves as the polling station for Wards 4 and 10 in the City of Beaver Dam. The day before elections, City workers set up the voting booths, tables, voting machines, and other equipment for the election. Poll workers come in the next morning. Voters visit the Center and cast their ballots. Upon returning to the Center the day after the election, all vestiges of the polling place are gone; and the Center is again a buzz of activity with Senior Center programming.

Remodeling and Renovation in the Giving Years

Parking Lot Expansion into Senior Center Property—1993

Over the objections of the Senior Center Director, Ann Neumaier; the Senior Center Steering Committee; and Senior Center members, the Common Council on a vote of 9 to 5 approved the linking of the Senior Center and Library parking lots in September 1993. This created 39 more parking stalls and expanded the Library onto Senior Center property.

A letter was sent to the Common Council signed by 172 senior citizens opposing this expansion. The senior community objected because of safety issues and the loss of Senior Center property. With the expansion, the Senior Center driveway used for access to the Library went right past the east entrance to the Senior Center.

The Council felt that this would not be a problem as the Senior Center would be closed when the Library traffic would increase. However, the senior citizens voiced concern that safety was an issue during the hours of 3:30 to 5:00 when middle school students were released and traffic intensified. The Center was still open during this time.

Seniors contended that they had already made allowances to the Library. Previously, a gate had been placed in the fence between the two facilities, and the Center had agreed to let library customers use the Senior Center lot.

In addition, 30 percent of the garden space for gardens was eliminated (10 to 12 gardens). Seniors objected to losing their garden plots and having to harvest their crops by Labor Day.

Seniors felt that an exit to North Spring Street was there for Library use and was a safer alternative. Because the railroad track was thought to be abandoned the next year, the seniors thought that the project could wait a year until the decision regarding the railroad track was made. However, the project was approved by the Common Council, despite the protests, at a cost not to exceed $24,000.

Remodeling the Interior Rooms—1997-1998

The Senior Center was extensively remodeled starting in February 1997. Delores Hagen, Rose Jarogoske, Jim Rollins, Al Schultz, Rita Spangler, Kaye Janisch, Al Tucker, and Director, Jana Stephens, served on the Remodeling Committee. Steering Committee members Anne Gartland, Josephine Rake, Marion Radtke, Mary Reilley, Mabel Schley, and Bill Hollihan assisted the Remodeling Committee. Jim Rollins, a construction retiree, volunteered his time for staining and varnishing the woodwork and a multitude of other tasks. Other volunteers from the Center also helped.

The service counter was removed from the main room. New carpet, wallpaper, and curtains were placed in the main room. Cupboards were placed by the kitchen area. The entryway into the dining room (which was also an outside entrance to the parking lot) became an Emergency exit. A new vinyl tile floor was placed in the kitchen. The Ceramics room was enlarged and received new lighting. The rest rooms were improved with new ceiling tiles, wallpaper, and mirrors. A utility storage room was created across from the men's rest room. The entry way into the Main Room was modified. The Center was closed for two weeks in January for the final remodeling effort. The cost of the project was covered by $18,000 from the Langmack estate, $6,000 from the City budget (cost of new flooring), and several thousand from the Project Account.

Removing the Service Counter that was a part of the original
building when it was purchased in 1973

Removing vestibule for an emergency exit

Installing the new cupboards by the kitchen

Making room for the kiln and remodeling the Ceramics room

Other Remodeling Projects

1. <u>1992</u>: A separate <u>storage facility</u> was built on the second floor by Floyd Schreiber and Bob Jeske.
2. <u>1993</u>: The Center was rewired. The City provided $5500 to cover the cost.
3. <u>1998</u>: A new phone system was installed. People were able to be paged. Phones were placed in the kitchen, game room, and office area.
4. <u>1999</u>: <u>New signage</u> was placed on the front lawn of the Center identifying the building. New carpeting was placed in the Pool Room. The building was <u>tuck pointed, sealed, and painted</u>.
5. <u>2000</u>: An <u>exhaust fan</u> was installed in the Ceramics Room. The <u>wall was extended in the Pool Room</u>.
6. <u>2001</u>: <u>Four electric doors</u> were added at the entrances for handicap accessibility.

Purchasing the House Next Door

In 1993, the Center Steering Committee considered buying the house next door to the Center. The house would have been torn down to expand parking. The cost of the house was $49,500. The City and the Library would not support this idea.

Parking Lot Renovation in 2003

The Center lot north of the building was to be renovated for additional parking in 2003. Buildings and a railroad bed were razed to construct this renovation.

The storage shed that had housed the van was still on the north end of the property, although van transportation had stopped sometime in 1997. The shed was now being used by the woodshop to store lumber, and some of the floats for various parades had been constructed there. The railroad tracks had been removed, but the railroad bed remained.

An extensive renovation of the parking lot occurred providing an <u>access road</u> to the Senior Center and Library that was placed over the old railroad bed. A <u>grassy boulevard</u> was placed between the access road and the parking lot. The Senior Center parking lot driveway was changed so it did not go right past the east entry.

The <u>storage shed was removed</u> in June 2003 to make more parking spaces. In November 2003, <u>nine trees were planted to line the driveway</u>. Plants and shrubs were added to the green space next to the building. The <u>flower bed and flag pole</u> were added at this time. This was the final parking lot renovation and how a visitor sees the configuration today when attending the Senior Center.

The Woodshop Gets a New Storage Shed

The woodshop guys needed a place to store their lumber, so a new shed was purchased in 2003. It took men to give directions and a Deere to get the shed in place behind the Senior Center. It is still there today.

The directions and the Deere

It Wasn't All Seriousness in the Giving Years

There was still time for special events and social activities in the Giving Years. Now let's take some time to describe them.

Beaver Dam Sesquicentennial

The Sesquicentennial was celebrated in 1991. A big celebration occurred on May 25, 1991, when there was a parade and events scheduled all over the city of Beaver Dam. Anne Gartland and Marion Radtke served as chairs for the Senior Center celebration to commemorate this event. The Senior Center celebrated by having an old-time ice cream social and volunteers dressed in old-time costumes. Homemade ice cream was made with an ice cream maker.

Geraldine Keel and Walter Wollin mixing ice cream

The Renaissance Band (Ye Queens Court Minstrels) performed at the Center, volunteers sold ice cream cones, and the Senior Center float proudly moved along the parade route.

Beaver Dam Senior Citizen float for the Sesquicentennial—
Marion Radtke and George Milton rode on the float

Tomato Growing Contest

Contestants grew their tomatoes at home or on garden plots at the Senior Center. The categories were largest, smallest most uniformly shaped, largest most uniformly shaped, first ripe, largest ripe, and most unusually shaped. There was a tomato growing contest in 1991, 1992, 1994, and 1995.

Tomato growers: (left to right) Emma Schultz,
Rachel Zuehlke, Alvin Schultz, Marion Radtke

The history shows the winners in 1991 and 1994. Here are the winners.

1991: Largest: 1) Rachel Zuehlke 2) Alvin Schultz 3) Marion Radtke. Smallest Most Uniformly Shaped: 1) Harlan Bogenschneider 2) Orval Gutgesell 3) Marion Radtke. Most Unusually Shaped: 1) Harlan Bogenschneider 2) Bernard Bashynski 3) Orval Gutgesell. Largest Most Uniformly Shaped: 1) Orval Gutgesell 2) Rachel Zuehlke 3) Orval Gutgesell. First Ripe: Linda Greeler. Smallest Ripe: 1) Marion Radtke 2) Linda Greeler 3) Hubert Turner. Largest Ripe: 1) Hubert Turner 2) Frieda Anton 3) Hubert Turner.

1994: First Ripe: Linda Greeler. Largest Ripe: Loraine Ackley. Most Uniformly Shaped: Verne Horne. Most Unusually Shaped: Hubert Turner.

Strawberry Feast

The first celebration of the strawberry season occurred in June of 1994. The Center celebrated with a strawberry shortcake feast.

There were volunteer pickers and pluckers. Pickers went to the strawberry fields and picked the strawberries. The pluckers plucked the stems from the strawberries. What is the best way to pluck a strawberry stem? Pluck the stem from the strawberry with a straw—push the straw through the bottom of the strawberry and push the stem outward.

Others mashed the strawberries, mixed them with sugar, baked the shortcake, and put the strawberries and ice cream on the shortcake the day of the feast.

Senior Expo

The first recorded date that the Senior Center participated in the Senior Expo was May 7, 1998. The Senior Center has continued to participate each year since that date. Volunteers have an opportunity to highlight Senior Center programs, activities, and special projects. Usually the Center provide a door prize. Volunteers man the booth for two-to four-hour stretches.

Manning the booth in front of Frebers at the
Beaver Dam Mall—Marna Bowe and Evelyn Beske—1998

Monthly Birthday Parties and Anniversaries

The birthdays of Senior Center members have always been celebrated at the Center. In 1996, the decision was made to have monthly birthday parties with cake and ice cream. The party occurs after bingo. A group picture is taken of the people who have birthdays each month, and the picture is displayed at the Center for that month. At a later date, anniversaries were added. The parties continue to the present day.

Celebrating in JuLy
Vi (& Paul) Hoffmann, Ruth (& Don) Hiley, Loretta Kasper, Linda Greeler, Mary & Russ Reilley

Birthday People for July

It's Movie Time

Movies have been a constant form of entertainment at the Center. Throughout the 90s, movies were shown monthly. Beginning in October 2002, movies were shown on Friday afternoons called "It's Movie Time."

A movie coordinator was sought in 2003. Kay Appenfeldt, a movie collector with over 500 movies in her collection, agreed to host the movies on Friday afternoon. Movies were Oscar classics, newly released movies, and Oscar contenders from the current or previous Oscar years. Movies goers participated in parties for Halloween and Christmas. In order to participate in the contest for a potential prize, the contestant had to view the movie for that day.

Yearly Halloween parties included contests in pumpkin carving, decorating a broom, and the best costume. Prizes were awarded.

At Christmas, movie goers could expect to receive something home baked and a present from Santa.

The big event—an Oscar party was held each year. Those attending the Oscar party had to predict the Oscar winners. They filled out a special Oscar form predicting who would win each category for the Academy Awards that year. Prizes were awarded to the persons with the most guesses correct after the Academy Award broadcast. Kay continued as the movie coordinator in 2009 and 2010.

Lunch Daze

Beginning in 2002, a special lunch program called Lunch Daze began. Only those who signed up for lunch could participate. Here is an example of activities for the month of October 2002. October 4: Best Smile Day; October 11 Teddy Bear Day (bring a Teddy Bear to lunch); October 14: Columbus Day (Trivia Contest); October 24: United Nations Day (wear a great hat). This continued each month through 2002 and 2003. Prizes were awarded.

Donations Given to the Senior Center

Special individuals or organizations have given donations to the Senior Center. Their gifts provided funds for remodeling the Center, offered entertainment to the Senior Center members, supported conservation, and established an endowment fund. Their thoughtfulness will forever be remembered.

Wings Over Wisconsin

Wings Over Wisconsin is a nonprofit conservation group which protects the habitat of pheasants and maintains the pheasant population in Dodge County and the surrounding area. Each year the organization brings bird seed to the Center as a drop off site. The bird seed is free to citizens to help feed the bird population in Beaver Dam in the winter time. The limit is one ice cream pail per customer in a given day. This has continued yearly since 1987. A donation was always welcomed.

Dart ball Boards/Dart ball League

The first dartball board was donated by Lyle Winker and First Lutheran Church in 1994. Dartball leagues were soon formed.

The Dart ball League

In 1995, the dart ball team winners were Jan Nickerson, Ed Raschka, Ruth Tucker, Art Wallendal, Arline Immerfall, Marion Radtke, Eve Hussli, and Orval Gutgesell.

In 1997, the dart ball team winners were Eve Hussli, Marion Radtke, Mitz Raschka, Ed Raschka, Jerry Klessing, Dan Urban, Joan Urban, Al Schultz, and Glen Yagodinski.

In 1999, the dart ball team winners were Geraldine Keel, Harvey Schoeffel, Ed Raschka, Mitz Raschka, Rich Krahenbuhl, Norma Krahenbuhl, Hilmer Diels, Al Tucker, Ruth Tucker, Bob Jeske, Jack Schmidt, Marion Radtke, Hugo Bonack, Orval Gutgesell, Doris Schumacher, and Glen Yagodinski.

Electronic Dart ball Machine

In 2002, an electronic dart ball machine was donated by Tommy Cristea-Rist. The machine still resides in the Pool Room at the Center.

Evan Gagnon Print

In 1995, Evan Gagnon donated a bluebird print that he created and designed in the painting class at the Senior Center. It was entitled, "Beaver Dam Blue." He painted it to honor the seniors who volunteered to work on the bluebird house project. A bluebird is sitting atop an Anderson type bluebird house. The Senior Center gave

Gagnon a bluebird house and a butterfly house in return. The print hangs on the office wall by the east entry.

The Donated Stereo System and Lunch Time Music

The family of Anona Garczynski donated a stereo system in her memory to the Senior Center in 2000. In July 2002, Lynn Winkie began playing music using the stereo system. This provided a tuneful hour during lunch. Lynn was called "our own music man."

Ralph Bennett Memorial

Through this gift in 1994, the Center was able to purchase tape and a tape dispenser. Both were not to exceed $200. Both would be used for shipping birdhouses.

Summary of the Giving Years

The giving years had many forms. The stories in this section reflect the generosity of the spirit in giving and receiving. Thankfulness abounds—because giving brings great joy.

Monetary Donations of $5000 or More and the Endowment Fund

Sizable donations were given by generous benefactors beginning with Ann Rogers Pfeffer. See her story on previous pages in this book.

The Steering Committee in January 2002 made the decision to purchase and engrave individual plaques for individuals donating $5000 or more to the Beaver Dam Senior Center.

The plaques that have been created are for the following individuals.

1996:   Evelyn and Ray Langmack
        Estate $30,000

1999:   The Martin Lutzke estate donation $10,000.

2001:   Robert F. Sackett donation of $23,790.93.

2004:   Vi Schneider (former Mayor of Beaver Dam) $10,637.07

2009:   Ervin and Marjorie Schulz
        $10,000 ($2000 specified for an electric wheelchair).

Endowment Fund

An endowment fund was established in 1996 after the Langmack donation. Resolution 146-96, a Resolution adopting the policy for donated funds to the Senior Citizen Center not specifically designated for current expenditures was adopted by the Common Council members on July 18, 1996. The Resolution is on file in the Archives of the Beaver Dam Senior Center.

Capital Improvement Resolution

An anonymous benefactor donated $350,000 to the Beaver Dam Senior Center in 2007.

Resolution 8-2008, a Resolution acknowledging receipt of donated funds and establishment of an account for the sole purpose of capital improvements at the Beaver Dam Senior Center was adopted on January 21, 2008 in recognition of this donation. The Common Council adopted the resolution with a unanimous vote. The Resolution is on file in the Senior Center Archives.

MONETARY DONATIONS
$100-$4999

Monetary donations of $100 to $4999 were also to be recognized. The Steering Committee in January 2002 established that a plaque should represent these donations. The plaque was bought from Beaver Dam Trophy for $144. It is made of American Walnut and has brass plates. Names are placed on the brass plates.

Those names of the plaque are:

AARP Local Chapter 1005

Lynn Winkie

In Memory of Robert Starker

In Memory of Oscar Mellenthin

In Memory of Dick Helbing

In Memory of Florence Hussli

In Memory of Robert Gloe
Smile Clinic of Manitowoc

Lynn Winkie
Toy Car Donation

In Memory of Alice Greinke

In Memory of Lawrence Koeppen

Individual plaques for donations $5000 or more

Plaque for monetary donations of $100 to $49999

SPECIAL STORIES FROM THE GIVING YEARS

A Large Screen TV. The 60-inch television was purchased in 2002. It has served as a source to play movies, watch sporting events, for Packer parties on Sunday, for exercise classes, or just to enjoy a favorite television program. It has been one of the most used sources of entertainment at the Center.

Jewels of the Blue. Don Kopff made two special video tapes of bluebirds. The first is called Jewels of the Blue—the second is a Kopff Bird Tour. They were made in 1992 and are still in the Archives at the Senior Center.

How Talented Are We. A talent show was held at the Senior Center in 1992. There was an afternoon of entertainment without competition. You could attend the event free if you performed; otherwise, the fee was $1.50. John Dentinger, a guest comedian performed. A film of this event is stored in the Archives.

Colored Newsletter. The newsletter was published in a different color each month starting in 1991. In addition, advertisers bought advertising on the pages for the first time.

Roaster Business. Lois Mietzel donated a roaster to be used for chili dinners.

Clavinova. Marna Bowe played the clavinova from 11 to 1 on Tuesday and Thursday. The Clavinova still resides at the Center.

Eye Study. The Eye Study hosted by the Beaver Dam Community Hospital held its first meeting in February of 1998 and began in March. The Eye Study has now asked the second generation to participate—the sons and daughters of the original eye study participants.

Another Coffee Story. The Steering Committee determined in February of 1998 that the coffee would be free to individuals who were working as a volunteer at the Center. Otherwise, a donation of 25 cents was requested.

Soda Anyone. The Coke machine in the back room arrived in 1999.

Tour Registration. In 1998, registration for tours was on a first-come first-serve basis. A payment in full was requested in order to guarantee a reservation. Also, a current health history was filled out and put on file at the Center.

Game Days. Friday afternoons were designated as Game Days. Board games of Scrabble, Chess, Chinese Checkers, Dominoes, Bowl and Score were available for seniors. This started in February 2001.

Cora Moylan. Cora served on the Steering Committee as the Park and Recreation Department liaison. She was supportive of older adults and Senior Center objectives. On April 26, 1995, the Center held a special recognition day for her dedication to the Center.

Lake Days Bingo. In 1997, 1998, and 1999, the Senior Center volunteers chaired by Mary Reilley ran a bingo event at Lake Days in Beaver Dam.

Greenhouse Bonanza. The highest amount of money in the Greenhouse account was in 1994. The account total was $10,247.93.

You Can't Beat the Price. The Steering Committee approved purchasing 900 two-inch pieces of cedar lumber in 1994. The cost was 35 cents each for a total of $315.

Business and Industry Booth. The rental of the booth in November of 1994 at the Business and Industry Days was considered a success. The visibility of the Senior Center was priceless.

The Kestrel Trail. Still visible today are the kestrel houses that Don Kopff and Julian Buss constructed for a kestrel trail. Those houses are on the east side of Hwy 151 going toward Sun Prairie. As the bluebird houses were placed on the highway to give nesting to the bluebirds, the kestrel houses were placed on the opposite side of the highway for the same purpose. Take a look at them the next time you travel to Columbus or Madison.

Painting the Trail. Norma and Rich Krahenbuhl painted the bluebird houses on the trail to Sun Prairie day after day until they were finished. Then Don Kopff thought the houses should be replaced with another bluebird nesting design. So Norma and Rich tagged the new houses with metal tags day after day until that task was done. Hope they treated themselves to ice cream or some other special treat when they were done each day.

Is There an Elephant in the Room? Try this for your large group meetings. Elephant Stew. 1 medium sized elephant, 2 rabbits (optional) Cut elephant into bite size pieces. Cover with brown gravy. Cover and simmer on kerosene stove at 475 degrees for 3-1/2 weeks. It should be enough to feed 3800 people. If more people show, add two rabbits. Be careful though, because some people don't like hare in their stew. (Reprinted from September 1983 Beaver Tales)

Recycling. The effort to recycle began at the Center in 1994.

<u>Equipment Purchased.</u> The divider panel that divides the main room for multiple events was purchased in September of 2003. The white board was purchased in 1997. The digital piano was purchased in 1995 for $1700.

<u>A Birthday Gift.</u> For his birthday each year, Bill Milarch donated cake and ice cream for all to enjoy.

<u>Bluebird T-shirts.</u> The Senior Center Woodshop had their own T-shirts made to support the Bluebird Restoration project.

Arnold Schroeder and Florence Mielke model the T-shirts

JANA STEPHENS
1996-1999

Jana came to the job with experience in parks and recreation. She had a Master's Degree in Park and Recreation Administration.

Jana grew up near Monroe. She spent five summers with the Monroe Park and Recreation Department and interned at the Monroe Senior Center.

Her experience included Camp, Family, and Youth Director at the YMCA in Winona, Minnesota.

Jana made intergenerational activities a priority while at the Senior Center. Many intergenerational programs were instituted. Brownie Badge projects, Pioneer groups building birdhouses, and a Seconds and Seniors reading program were among those developed.

Computer classes were offered to the senior community at the Beaver Dam Middle School, Beaver Dam High School, and Jefferson School. Most computer classes were intergenerational. Participation at the Senior Expo started, and monthly birthday parties with cake and ice cream occurred after Bingo.

Jana was instrumental in obtaining the funds from the Langmack estate for extensively remodeling the Center. The service counter was removed, cupboards were placed in the kitchen area, entryways were changed, improvements were made to walls and floors, rest rooms were renovated, and a utility storage room was built.

Taxi service for Senior Center members began, and the Endowment fund was established.

Jana resigned in April 1999 to accept a position at the City of Beaver Dam Parks and Recreation Department.

AMY PALM
1999-2002

Amy joined the Senior Center as Director in September of 1999.

Amy graduated with a Bachelor of Science degree in English from University of Wisconsin Stevens Point. She received a Master's Degree in Gerontology from St. Cloud State in Minnesota. Amy worked at the regional senior center in St. Cloud.

Her experience included a summer camp for older adults in Pennsylvania, and a retired and senior volunteer program in Dane County.

Under her directorship, the Book Club and Genealogy group began. AARP meetings were conducted at the Center, and game days were instituted. The computer lab opened, and computer classes were taught on site.

The age requirement for joining the Senior Center was lowered, and the toy project and Christmas cars were born in the Woodshop.

Amy was instrumental in beginning the accreditation self study with the Wisconsin Association of Senior Centers. The Center was initially accredited in July of 2001.

She wanted education and fitness for seniors. Amy felt that senior activities are not limited to the building where a senior center is headquartered.

THE RECENT YEARS
2004-2010

We will take a walk down memory lane and randomly tell the stories of the members, volunteers, projects, and activities that we remember from the past seven years. Hopefully, they will bring a smile to your face or jog a memory of a special day for you.

Reaccreditation with the Wisconsin Association of Senior Centers (WASC)

How proud we were to be reaccredited by WASC in August of 2006. A special banquet at Dos Gringos was held in September of 2006 to celebrate the event. Those in attendance were members of the WASC evaluating panel, the Senior Center Director, Steering Committee members, and reaccredidation committee members.

The accreditation process is a self study of an individual senior center. The Beaver Dam Senior Center was re-evaluated by Senior Center members beginning in 2005. Twenty categories were studied by the reaccredidation committee. Members were Don Jacob, Darwin Bremer, Dwayne Braun, Mary Ann Hussli, Rita Spangler, Kay Appenfeldt, and Senior Center Director, Evonne Koeppen.

The categories studied were mission, goals, governing documents, structure, governing body, advisory board, community resources, public information, community planning, program, evaluation, administration, personnel polices and procedures, emergency procedures, budget fiscal management, risk protection, records and reports, confidentiality, and facility. Each category is thoroughly investigated and a summary is written for each based on WASC guidelines. Goals and guiding principles are also written for each category.

The Committee compiled their research of the categories in an Accreditation Manual which was sent to WASC. A panel from WASC evaluated the summaries and based on their evaluation awarded accreditation.

This study is instrumental in learning the strengths and weaknesses of your Senior Center.

When the Senior Center received the reaccreditation, the Center was one of only 22 that had been awarded this distinction in the state of Wisconsin.

WASC Accreditation 2001

The initial accreditation was received in July 2001. The self study was completed by the Steering Committee starting in the latter part of 2000. Members were Mary Reilley, Julian Buss, Bill Hollihan, Arlene (Silloway) Christian, Rich Krahenbuhl, Ron Andrews, Marion Radtke, Kathryn Barbour, and Al Tucker. Amy Palm, Senior Center Director, was instrumental in starting this process.

National Accreditation

The Senior Center Steering Committee approved seeking national accreditation with the National Institute of Senior Centers in 2005 and 2007. The National Institute is a unit of the National Council on the Aging, Inc. Circumstances prevailed and the studies were never started.

However in 2009, the Steering Committee once again approved seeking national accreditation. A Senior Center Accreditation Committee was formed. The members are Mary Morgan, Marion Radtke, Diane Fabini, Traci Gmeinder, Ellie Schoeffel, Kay Appenfeldt, Chair; and Evonne Koeppen, Administrator. They are actively self assessing the Senior Center and hope to have this project ready for submission to the national organization sometime in 2011.

Accreditation Committee. Seated (left to right) Mary Morgan, Ellie Schoeffel, Evonne Koeppen, Administrator; Kay Appenfeldt, Chair. Standing (left to right) Diane Fabini, Writer/Editor; Marion Radtke, Traci Gmeinder, Office Administrator who compiles the documentation and puts the Accreditation Manuals in final form
Not pictured: Nancy Wise

Third Reaccreditation by WASC

As the Accreditation Committee completed the research and documentation for National Accreditation, the Committee was also using that research to prepare the supporting documentation to seek reaccreditation for the third time from WASC. The Acccreditation manual was submitted to WASC at the end of June 2011. The Evaluation Committee from WASC came to the Senior Center on July 15, 2011. Each section was reviewed by the two WASC representatives and they provided advice and complimentary conclusions to the Accreditation Committee and Steering Committee members. The manual was complimented for its strength of purpose, the depth of its documentation, and conciseness. Several of the documents from the Senior Center Accreditation Manual will be used as examples to help other Senior Centers in the state achieve their accreditation.

The Center was awarded its third reaccreditation on that day. A formal presentation and the awarding of the plaque occurred at the WASC Convention on September 29, 2011.

In November 2011, Evonne Koeppen, Administrator, informed the City of Beaver Dam Common Council at its monthly meeting that the Beaver Dam Senior Center had received this reaccreditation. A celebratory event with a program and complimentary breakfast was held at the Senior Center on November 18, 2011. The event recognized the Accreditation Committee members from 2001, 2006, and 2011.

WASC Honorary Accreditation Plaque and Accreditation Book

Volunteer Presidential Awards

In April 2005, a special Presidential Award was presented to fourteen volunteers at the Senior Center. Each had completed 100 or more hours of voluntary service to the Senior Center. They received an award from the President of the United States. The Award is pictured on the next page.

Presented by the President's Council on Service

and Civic Participation to

BEAVER DAM SENIOR CENTER

in recognition and appreciation of your

commitment to strengthening our Nation and for

making a difference through volunteer service.

An initiative of the President's Council on Service and Civic Participation in conjunction with

Volunteer Presidential Award

Volunteer Receptionists

A volunteer receptionist manned a desk as you entered the east entryway into the Center in 2005. Her job was to greet visitors and remind them to sign in for the activities they were doing at the Center that day. This was done with volunteer logs that were hand written. Pearl Dobbratz served as one of the receptionists that sat at the desk. The desk was donated by Lynn Winkie when he retired from the Center. Later members signed in at the podium stand.

Computerized Attendance Tracking System

It was time to modernize the Center beginning in 2008. The Steering Committee authorized the purchase of computerized tracking system software called My Senior Center in August. The software and equipment was installed in October. What seems like a "sure thing" now was a stressful activity when it began.

Members receive a membership card. This membership card is scanned on the scanner to the computer each time a member comes to the Center. Their name then comes up on the computer screen. The activities for the day are printed on the screen. The member touches the screen for each activity they attend that day. Volunteer coordinators or volunteers can go to a separate screen to key in the hours for the events they attend or coordinate for that day.

The tracking system can then compute electronically the daily attendance for each program or event in a given day. Monthly reports can also be issued giving the Administrator valuable attendance records of Senior Center activity.

Jean Schulz and Richard Parker Sign In on the Computerized Tracking System

Fundraisers 2004-2009

Fundraisers have been the major means for funding the programs and activities for the Senior Center for 40 years. Monies earned from the fundraising projects replenish the Project Account/Senior Center Account, and this continues on a repetitive basis each year. Monies from this account are used to pay for the expenses that are paid to provide the programs and activities to the participants at the Senior Center.

2004 Fundraiser: October Fling. There were two sets of public bingo games of 10 games each held at the Center. Each started at a different time during the day. Hot beef and turkey sandwiches, chips, and homemade desserts were served. The raffle drawing was at 1:30. The grand prize was $500.

2005 Fundraiser: A Casino Party. For $5, gamblers received $1000 in funny money to play Blackjack, Roulette, Craps, Horse Racing, or Texas Hold 'Em. Modern Woodman matched the sales from the fundraiser up to $2000. For the first time, a raffle ticket book was sent to a compiled list of people from Beaver Dam. An enclosed letter asked the people to send the $5 back or bring it to the Senior Center. This was done in hopes of selling more tickets. The grand prize was a $250 gas card.

2006 Fundraiser. Harvest Masked Ball. This was the first fundraiser held at another locality. It was held at the Elks Club. The Too Sound Effects DJ provided the music and dancers took to the dance floor. A $150 set of dining coupons and a $150 gas card were the grand prizes. Raffle tickets were again sent in the mail.

2007 Fundraiser. Grandma's Attic, Silent Auction, and Fall Raffle. Center items no longer usable were sold. Center members were asked to bring items for the rummage sale. The computer room was filled with rummage items for sale The Main Room held the silent auction. Raffle tickets were again sent through the mail. The grand prize was $250 sponsored by Golden Living Center.

2008 Fundraiser. Baby Boomer Sock Hop. The Doo Wop Daddies, a 50s and 60s rock and roll group, sang for the bobby soxers who strolled, jitterbugged, and twisted the night away in October. Tickets were $10 before the event and $15 at the door. During the intermissions, contests were held for a hula hoop contest, a bubble gum blowing contest, a jitterbug dance contest, and a twist dance contest. Pictures were taken at a cutout of a sock hop couple

Sock Hop Couple Rita Spangler and Mayor Tom Kennedy

People who came dressed as for a sock hop received a prize. A bucket raffle ($1 a ticket or 6 for $5 or an arm's length for $20) occupied one side of the room. Two 50/50 raffles were held during the night. The grand prize was $100. The Dance Committee were Gert Miller, Darlene (Butter) Morissey, Kay Appenfeldt, and Evonne Koeppen. Helpers at the dance were Annie Nielsen, Sally Adam, Lorna Schultz, Del Schultz, Mary Morgan, Pauline Corning-Garvin, Marion Radtke, Terry Appenfeldt, and Rebecca Schultz.

Baby Boomer Sock Hop.—Oh we had fun!

<u>2009 Fundraiser.</u> Country Western Dance. The Whiskey River Band played in October at the Youth Building at the Dodge County Fairgrounds. Snowflakes were in the air on that day—we expected better weather in October. The dancers were chilled in the non-heated Youth Building but that didn't stop them from line dancing and cuddling close for the slow dances. Cow races (tickets $2), a lasso the steer horn contest ($2 for 5 tickets), paddles ($1 a paddle), and a heads or tails game were also played.

The cow races are ready to begin.

Terry Appenfeldt, Kay Appenfeldt, Darlene (Butter) Morrissey, and Mary Morgan served as the Dance Committee. Helpers at the dance were Rena Hughes, Jack Ulrich, Adminstrator, Evonne Koeppen, Larry Koeppen, Len Klawitter, Marion Radtke, Fiona and Chris Elvers, and Barb Klossner. The grand prize was $100. Tickets for the event were $15.

Country-western Dance Committee: (left to right) Terry Appenfeldt, Kay Appenfeldt, Darlene (Butter) Morrissey, Mary Morgan.

The Diner's Edge Coupon Book

Volunteers contacted local restaurants to participate in this offer. The restaurants offered special dinner offers which were printed in a coupon book. The book was called the Diner's Edge. The book sold for $15. Leaders Wayne Schmitz and Del Schultz put together this fundraiser in 2008 and 2009.

Senior Center Account and Its Formats

The Project Account has been called a series of names since 1974. However, it purpose has remained the same. The funds which enter this account are used to pay for activities, for programs, and for events specifically for the Senior Center.

The first accounts were the coffee funds, the Refreshment Fund, and the Sunshine Account. The funds from each of them paid for social activities at the Center in the 1970s.

In 1975, the Senior Center Account emerged. The Center volunteers were generating money from fundraising events, and those monies needed to be funneled into an account.

In 1995, there were three separate accounts: Greenhouse, Birdhouse Sales, and the Senior Center Account. This continued until around 1998 or 1999. The Project Account then emerged to house all the funds. The endowment fund has been in place since 1996.

When the 2005-2006 reaccreditation study occurred, there were three accounts: the Senior Center account, the Travel account, and the Endowment fund. That continues today. The Senior Center account handles monies for income earned for programs and activities at the Center. The Travel account houses monies to support tours, day trips, and extended trips. The endowment fund remains as it was instituted in 1996. The endowment funds are protected by two separate Resolutions insuring that the monies are used for the Senior Center.

The Senior Center Account is managed by the Steering Committee Treasurer, Senior Center Office Administrator, and the Administrator. Two signatures are required to withdraw money from the Senior Center account. The Steering Committee treasurer, Senior Center Office Adminstrator, and Administrator can sign the checks.

Monies that are funneled into the Senior Center Account are from birdhouse sales, cookie sales, greenhouse sales, fundraisers/raffles, card parties and any other Senior Center program or activity that earns money. The Senior Center account summary is presented monthly to the Steering Committee and is audited annually.

The Travel Account is managed by the Administrator and Senior Center Office Administrator. It is also audited annually.

Building rental, class fees, newsletter subscriptions, and sales tax amounts are forwarded to the City budget. The City budget pays for maintenance of the building, heating and electricity, water, and City employee salaries.

Donations Come in Many Formats

May 2005. Dick Helbing donated $622 to the Center to be used for the card players. Three card tables were purchased.

June 2007. Doug Randall donated several tools to the woodshop.

October 2007. Chuck Yagodinski donated new billiard balls for the Pool Room in memory of his father, Glen Yagodinski.

October 2007. Alice Engebretson donated an American flag to the Senior Center.

Jim Bahls, Beaver Dam Shoe Repair, hung grommets in the entry closet to hang exercise mats at his expense.

November 2009. Larry Neitzel donated 400 feet of walnut and apple wood to the Senior Center Woodshop. Larry additionally donated woodworking tools, a planer/joiner, and woodworking supplies.

June 2009. Bunny Schmidt donated woodworking tools to the Senior Center Woodshop in honor of her husband, Jack Schmidt.

Fall 2009. Terry Zimmerlee who represented the Lions Club of Beaver Dam donated a reader to assist those who have handicapped eyesight.

November 2009. Friends of the Beaver Dam Community Center donated a DVD player and VIZIO HDTV to the Center. The TV was donated to Friends by Wal-Mart.

November 2009. Kathy Christensen donated $100 in memory of her father, Eugene Zarling, who enjoyed playing cards and making friends at the Center. She suggested the money be used for the Christmas party that year.

Others have donated gas mileage, time, and labor to the various projects and programs offered at the Senior Center.

Woodshop in the Recent Years

The Woodshop was without a coordinator after Jim Schwartz resigned in 2005. However, volunteer Ken Hardinger made sure the Christmas cars were made for the Christmas parade in 2006. In 2007, Terry Appenfeldt accepted the position of Woodshop Manager.

Beaver Dam Lake Property Owners Banquet

The Beaver Dam Lake Property Owners banquet occurs each year in March. The Senior Center has donated items for the auction for this banquet for ten years or more. Items donated have come primarily from the Senior Center Woodshop.

In 2008, Louis Terlisner designed a boat replicating "The Rambler," which was an excursion steamship on Beaver Dam Lake in the 1900s. He created his design from looking at a historical decorative plate designed by Frank Mittlestadt which depicted the Rambler on Beaver Dam Lake. This became the donated auction item from the Center in 2008.

Lewis Terlisner and replicated "Rambler"

In 2009, a plate shelf was designed by Terry Appenfeldt as the auction item for the banquet. The shelf holds the ten historical plates designed by Frank Mittlestadt. The plates depict scenes from Beaver Dam history and are the gift that sponsors receive for supporting the Lake Property Owners Association. The Center has received an artistic Frank Mittlestadt collector plate each year from the auction items that are donated and those are display at the Center.

The Plate Shelf for Beaver Dam Lake Property Owners Association Banquet

Wings Over Wisconsin Banquet

The Wings Over Wisconsin banquet is held each year in February. Each year the Senior Center donates a gift for that banquet. Usually that gift comes from the Senior Center Woodshop.

In 2008, Terry Appenfeldt built a Cody Cruiser for the banquet. A Cody Cruiser is a toy upon which a child two to four years old can ride.

Cody Cruiser

In 2009, a clock was presented to Wings Over Wisconsin for the banquet. The clock design was done on a woodcarving machine by Harold Ninneman.

In 2010, Lewis Terlisner and Terry Appenfeldt designed and constructed an 8-gun free standing glass and wood gun cabinet.

Wings Over Wisconsin presents the Center with a wildlife print each year—honoring the Center as being a sponsor for the organization. Those prints are on display at the Center.

BRAW (Bluebird Restoration Association of Wisconsin

The Association rents the Senior Center for their nestbox seminar. The first event was March 13, 2004. Informational seminars, guest speakers, and displays characterize the all day event. At that first nestbox seminar, Jim Schwartz, Bill Christian, and Ken Hardinger helped children build bluebird houses.

Nestbox seminars continued in 2005, 2006, 2007, and 2009. The seminars featured speakers and displays consistent with helping the bird population specifically the bluebird. The Senior Center Woodshop opened its doors to sell bluebird nesting boxes and kits, wood duck houses, wren kits, and martin houses. Woodshop volunteers Terry Appenfeldt, Jack Ulrich, and Ken Hardinger built bluebird houses with children and were available to discuss construction and design of their projects.

Kestrel Houses

Barb Harvey, local raptor conservationist, contracted with the Beaver Dam Senior Center Woodshop in 2007 to build kestrel houses. Ken Hardinger was the primary builder of the kestrel houses and also volunteers in the Woodshop for a multitude of other activities.

Ken Hardinger

Artic Tip ups

Artic Tip Ups, a local manufacturer of an ice fishing tip up, contracted with the Beaver Dam Senior Center in 2009 to make the blanks for the tip ups. The woodshop guys Robert Horne, Harvey Schoeffel, Len Klawitter, Lewis Terlisner, Rich Krahenbuhl, Ken Hardinger, and Terry Appenfeldt busily cut holes, route, and plane the blanks. An order went out weekly.

Robert Horne (background); Len Klawitter (forground)
working on a Woodshop project

Presentation Plaques for the City of Beaver Dam

Woodshop guys, Terry Appenfeldt and Ken Hardinger, made presentation plaques for Mayor Tom Kennedy for the City of Beaver Dam. One set was used to give presentation plaques to the owners of ten buildings that were razed during the downtown demolition in 1999. The other plaques will be used as presentation plaques to recognize City employees.

Special Projects from the Woodshop 2007-2010

The woodshop guys built pier sections for local customers, delivered them, and installed them on Beaver Dam Lake.

Other items constructed were Civil War reenactment chairs, a picnic table, a dining room table, a parlor table, book shelves for the front office, wood duck houses, suet hanging bird feeders, angel houses, flower pot hangers, large, medium, and small bird feeders, thistle bird feeders, martin houses, newsletter folding jigs, letters/ numbers for Keith's Barber Shop, Pom Pom makers, squirrel feeders, frames for puzzles, and the woodshop display cabinet.

Numerous small repair projects were completed by the Woodshop guys for a multitude of people. By repairing the item, it helped the individual to keep that repaired item for several more years.

Woodshop guys. (left to right) Lewis Terlisner, Ken Hardinger, Woodshop Manager Terry Appenfeldt, Wayne Gibbs, Darrell Kalmes Not pictured Robert Horne, Len Klawitter, Orville Sette, Harvey Schoeffel

Recognition Awards from the Senior Center Woodshop

The following recognition awards were all handcrafted in the Center Woodshop. In June 2008, a wooden handcrafted plaque was presented to Katy Frank-Randall on behalf of her husband Doug. Doug Randall donated multiple tools to the Woodshop. The plaque hangs on the Woodshop wall.

Terry Appenfeldt presents Katy Frank-Randall with the bluebird house plaque

In June 2008, a Cody Cruiser was presented to Chad Abel from Northwoods. His company donates most of the wood that the Woodshop uses to construct its projects. The Cody Cruiser was made from the wood that he donated.

In March 2009, a handcrafted wooden movie reel projector was presented to Noah Wheeler and Debbie Lorenz from Family Video. Family Video donates the rental of the movies for the Movie Club at the Senior Center.

In September 2009, a set of wooden handcrafted steer horns was presented to John Moser of WBEV/WXRO radio. The radio station donated multiple dollars of free promotional ads for both the Baby Boomer Sock Hop and the Country Western dance.

Those recognition awards are important. They thank the business owners and major contributors for their contribution. In all cases, each has provided a valuable service to the Senior Center; and it was the Senior Center's way to say thank you. All were designed by Terry Appenfeldt with assistance from the woodshop guys.

Wal-Mart Fall Cleanup Project

Each year starting in 2006, Wal-Mart employees assist seniors with fall cleaning activities. They rake leaves, clean gutters, and other fall cleanup activities. For the Senior Center participation, Wal-Mart pays the Senior Center for the wages of the Wal-Mart people who participate in this charitable activity. The Center has received a cleanup project check yearly since the event began.

Intergenerational Activities in the Recent Years

Grandparents Day

On September 12, 2004, Grandparents Day was held at the Senior Center. A letter was sent from the Center to Day Care Centers in the City of Beaver Dam. The letter asked children to bring their grandparents to the Center. That day they played old fashioned games, made bird houses, had their faces painted, took photos, and made a grandparent's card. They also made potato jewelry. Wal-Mart generously funded the day. Grandparent's Day continues annually.

Community Care Day Care

The Kids from Community Care Day Care came to the Center in 2005. Leaders Mary Hollihan, Rich Krahenbuhl, Ken Hardinger, and Bill Hollihan helped children build birdhouses. Each child took their constructed birdhouse home in a brown paper bag.

Flag Day Ceremony

On Flag Day, June 14, 2005, children from the Rainbow Connection Day Care came to the Center during a Flag Day Ceremony. Seniors assisted children to write cards and letters to PFC Kevin Braaksma and his unit in Iraq. A youth group, Rascals and Rockers sang patriotic songs.

Rita Spangler (left) and Ellie Schoeffel (right) assisting the children to write letters

Kids Care Comes to the Center

The Kids Care Day Care Center came to the Center on June 13 and June 20, 2006. Arvid Behm, Mary Hollihan, Ken Hardinger, and Bill Hollihan helped the children to build birdhouses.

Mary Hollihan assisting a student to build a birdhouse

Woodcarvers and Soap Carving

Don Jacob and volunteer woodcarvers took their carving skills to 4H clubs. They taught 4H children how to carve soap in 2005 and 2006.

Beaver Dam Area Arts Association—Arts in the Park

John and Marge Haider, Terry and Kay Appenfeldt, and Ken Hardinger sold bluebird and wren kits at the Seippel Arts Center on a beautiful day in October 2007. After the kit was purchased, the team assisted the children to build the birdhouse.

Recreation Programs In the Park

As a part of the summer recreation program in 2008, children enrolled in a program to spend an afternoon at Waterworks Park in Beaver Dam doing various summertime activities. One of the activities was to build a birdhouse. Terry and Kay Appenfeldt and John and Marge Haider assisted the children. The children all signed a birdhouse and gave it back to the Center.

Building Time With Grandmas and Grandpas

Volunteer coordinator Marge Haider organized activities for children from Jefferson School. A staff of volunteers Marion Radtke, Annie Nielsen, Terry Appenfeldt, John Haider, Shirley and Keith Grotjohn, and Don Jacob assisted with the weekly activities. The program was created in conjunction with a program called 21st Century Community Learning Center.

The students came to the Senior Center to interact with older adults in the fall of 2008. Over a several week span, the children played bingo and games, toured the Library, did exercise and nutrition, and learned about orioles and built an oriole feeder in conjunction with volunteers from the Senior Center Woodshop.

Marge and John Haider with children from Jefferson School

Dodgeland School Career Day

Woodshop volunteers Ken Hardinger and Rich Krahenbuhl went to Dodgeland Schools to build birdhouses with school children in 2009. This is a continuing activity.

Charter School and the Woodshop

Terry Appenfeldt and Darrell Kalmes taught woodworking skills to Charter students starting in the fall of 2008. Darrell and Terry volunteered their time to teach the classes at the Charter School of the Beaver Dam Unified School District. They were pleased when they were invited to the graduation ceremony for those graduating in 2008. The program continued in 2009 and 2010.

Education at the Senior Center During the Recent Years

A multitude of different education opportunities were offered to the senior center participants. Some were through classroom instruction, some through a challenge to energize creativity, and some through informational speakers. All helped those who participated to learn something new or to energize their creative spirit.

Scandinavian Woodcarving. The woodcarvers called in a specialist carver in October 2004. The carvers learned to carve from Jim Hoeffer, instructor from Watertown. Members of the class were Duane Schroeder, Alyce Schoenwetter, Paul King, Louis Antonioni, Eric Huizenga, Harold Vanderhei, Don Jacob, and Jack Ramey.

Nutritional Kitchen Workshops. Cooking classes with nutritionist, Ellen Sushak, stress basic or special cooking skills and food preparation. Her first classes were called Healthy Holiday Foods and Bake and Take. Healthy nutrition is emphasized with each meal that is prepared. Classes are offered monthly, and Ellen uses different themes and foods for the meals prepared at each session. Ellen began Men's Cooking Classes in May of 2008.

Cooking Classes in Action. Standing Ellen Sushak, Nutritionist and Instructor

Leatherworking. Larry Neitzel volunteered to teach a leatherworking class beginning February 28, 2006.

Aerobics. An 8-week aerobics class started in April 2006.

<u>Video Art Lessons.</u> A technologically run class also began in April 2006. Via DVD instruction, members could receive art lessons.

<u>Spanish Language and Culture.</u> Starting May 15, 2006, a Spanish language and culture class was taught by Marge Haider and Hortensia Garcia.

<u>Computer Instruction.</u> Computer classes in Beginning and Advanced Computers and the Internet continued with instructors Barb Ludtke, Kay Appenfeldt, Bill Schassler, and Jack Hankes. Three new computers were purchased in August 2006.

<u>Breakfast for the Brain.</u> This class ran from February 9 to April 15, 2008. Participants met twice a week to increasingly more difficult exercises to stimulate the brain. The class goal was to stimulate measurable results in memory. Class members worked together, had discussions, and recalled memories together. The class was taught by Lori VandenHouten, Alzheimer Care Unit Director from Golden Living Center in Beaver Dam.

<u>Wood burning.</u> A Wood burning class began in April of 2009. Wood burning requires special equipment called wood burning tips. Students create their own designs from free hand or preprinted designs traced on wood. Artists wood burn those designs on wood by heating a variety of different sized tips, and the artist uses those tips to create decorative burn marks on wood. Many artistic pictures of eagles, country scenes, and animals were created by the members of the class.

The Computer Room was rewired to accommodate this class taught by Terry Appenfeldt. Marsha Horne, a talented wood burning artist, instructs the class today.

The Woodburning Class: Jack Ulrich, Carol Utrie, Alyce Schoenwetter, Harold Vanderhei, Paul King, Terry Appenfeldt, Instructor; Don Jacob, Larry Mielke, Bob Horne, Marsha Horne

Woodburning Art Plaque

The Wood burning class of 2010 decided to complete a class project—an art plaque. Marsha Horne devoted 37 hours to this project drawing the designs and wood burning. Terry Appenfeldt and Paul King assisted with the country theme which included scenes of nature. Marsha stated, "I have always admired the looks of wood burning. This project was the most challenging I have ever experienced." A frame of recycled barn board frame featuring a wooden maple leaf in each corner designed by Terry Appenfeldt compliments the artwork.

Marsha Horne and the country themed wood burning art plaque

Rise and Shine Breakfast

This program brought in informational speakers to update and educate the senior community. Committee members Kay Appenfeldt, Maxine Baumheier, Alice Engebretson, and Evonne Koeppen, Administrator, started the program in September of 2004. Their first speaker was Andy Strahota and Ali, K9 officers for the City of Beaver Dam Police Force.

The Committee contacted speakers, prepared promotional brochures, and arranged the programs on a monthly basis. Those that signed up ate breakfast prepared by Kay, Maxine, and Alice around 9:00. Breakfasts ($3-$3.50) ranged from breakfast casserole, pancakes, cinnamon rolls, muffins, eggs, bacon, and toast, biscuits and gravy, ham cakes, breakfast bars and sausages, and a variety of other delicious meals. Breakfast cookbooks were a staple in preparing for the program. The speaker's presentation started at around 9:30. When Maxine retired, Gert Miller joined the program. Later, programs met every other month.

Right Before Lunch

The Rise and Shine Breakfast became the Right Before Lunch program in April of 2009. When the participants evaluated the Rise and Shine Breakfast program, they felt the Rise and Shine Breakfast was too early in the morning and too close to lunch. The Committee met, listened to the participants, and created the program called Right Before Lunch.

Informational speakers still come to inform and educate. The first Right Before Lunch speaker was Beaver Dam Municipal Judge Ken Peters. The speaker's presentation is around 10:30, and those who wish to stay can take part in the Dodge County Nutritional Site luncheon. Four or five programs are planned per year. Kay, Alice, Gert, and Evonne continue to prepare the events for the year by contacting speakers and hosting the programs.

Writer's Group

Instructor, Denise Reschke, began the Writer's workshop in February 2003. Writers who wrote poetry, essays, parts to books, or a family history enrolled in the class.

John Patterson, a retired Wayland instructor, volunteered to instruct the group beginning in January 2004. John reviewed the writer's work and offered constructive ideas. John said, "They were so active and they were as sharp as the kids at Wayland."

Each read what they had written and all discussed how it could be improved. The class members learned from each other. The objective of the group is to experience the joy of writing.

There is no pressure to have a piece of work written for each class time. Betty Eilbes wrote short stories for her grandchildren. Ellie Schoeffel is a long-time poetry writer, and the author of the poem at the beginning of this history. Other members were Florence Rhodes, Roy Gentz, Joyce Gentz, and Beth Keitzman.

In January 2008, Karla Jensen became the new coordinator of the Writer's Group. The group begins each session writing a short story about a topic that Karla provides for them. Each reads their short story and receives complimentary comments from the others in class. Later Karla shares writing concepts or publishing information. During the second half of the session, individuals read their own written stories or poems for the group's feedback. A friendly and enjoyable group setting makes everyone feel comfortable in sharing their work. Karla will critique the work if asked to do so by the writer. The group meets twice a month; and for awhile during tax season in 2008, the Group met at City Hall for their sessions.

Writer's Group: Seated (left to right) Karla Jensen, Volunteer Coordinator; Glen Wiesmueller, Darlene Pieper, Mary Reak Standing (left to right) Margaret Marshall, Marguerite Van Hulst, Ann Hoekstra, Terry Henning, Florence Rhodes, Ellie Schoeffel. Not pictured Helen Wieczorek, Miriam Schyvinck, Laura Larson, Nancy Maleck

Remembering Then and Now

The Writer's Group compiled their individual pieces of work and submitted them to a publisher, and a book was published. The book was called Remembering Then and Now. A book signing party was held at the Senior Center on November 28, 2006. The book sells for $10 a copy

The Second Story

The Writer's Group continued to write short stories and poems. Their accumulated work has generated another book. The new book is called The Second Story The publication date is December 2010.

Remembering Then and Now and The Second Story

Exercising the Body During the Recent Years

This past section exercised the brain and presented challenges to improve the mind. This next section recognizes that older adults also want to exercise their bodies. The Senior Center accommodated with the following programs.

Arthritis Exercise

Mary Ann Hussli suggested that the Center initiate this class when she returned from Colorado. This type of arthritis class was offered in a Senior Center in the town where she vacations. Mary Ann with Ellen Sushak took certification classes to become certified instructors in arthritis exercise. The first arthritis exercise class began in January 2007.

Later, Mary Desjarlais also received certification training and has joined Mary Ann and Ellen as an instructor. Participants say they have more movement in joints, hands, and arthritic areas because of the exercises from this class. The class meets twice a week and continues today.

The Arthritis Class in Action: Left to Right (clockwise): Mary Desjarlais, Arthritis Exercise Instructor; Shirley Grotjohn, Nancy Guenther, Jackie Roedl, Jean Wellbeloved, Sandy Radke, Audrey Roedl, Rita Shesky, Elaine Wheeler, Ellen Sushak and Mary Ann Hussli, Arthritis Exercise Instructors Not pictured Carol Edmunds, Marge Lehmann, Darlene Wright, Marian Youngdale

Qi Gong

Qi Gong is an ancient Chinese method of exercise. It uses soft, flowing motions with deep breathing to heal the body and rid the body of tension. Qi Gong improves the immune system to help to ward off disease. The first class taught by Jean Hill from Beaver Dam Community Hospital began on November 2, 2004.

Snappy Steppers

A walking group formed in September 2004. They walked every Tuesday morning as a group, or individuals could join and walk on their own. Members recorded their mileage. Their first goal was to record their mileage and that mileage would accumulate enough miles to walk to Hawaii. The volunteer coordinator was Gloria Klug.

Poker Walk

The group formed after a Poker Walk in September 2004. Fifteen to sixteen walkers joined to walk one mile or two miles. Scheduled stops were set up at various businesses along the one-and two-mile walks. At each stop, a walker would pick up a playing card. The walkers with the best poker hand at the end of the walk received prizes. The walkers returned to the Senior Center where poker hands were displayed and prizes were awarded.

Polar Walk

On Tuesday, January 25, 2005, starting at 9 a.m., walkers walked the route of their choice. One or two-mile walks were done. Thaw out stations were along each walk. Walkers would pick up a card at the thaw out station and then continue walking. Mileage was tripled to help the walkers get to Hawaii. Prizes were awarded for the best poker hands.

Hawaiian Luau

The walkers completed their mileage to Hawaii in May of 2005. A Luau was held with all the appropriate food and fun. The walkers walked 5,464 miles.

National Senior Health and Fitness Day

The Snappy Steppers participated in this national day in May of 2005 with another Poker Walk. The routes were one-half mile, one mile, and two miles. The National Senior Health and Fitness Day is an annual event nationally. The goal is to energize seniors into regular physical activity. It is the nation's largest health promotion event for older adults.

Another Poker Walk was scheduled for this day on May 31, 2006. Volunteer coordinators were Edna Heinemeier and Lois Soboleski.

Seattle, Washington, and the Salmon Feed

The Snappy Steppers chose their next destination. They were walking to Seattle, Washington, a total of 1939.73 miles. Their goal was to arrive for a salmon feed. They did so in October 2005 by finishing one last Poker Walk of one-half, one, and two miles. The party followed and salmon highlighted the menu.

Programs Just for Fun in the Recent Years

Some programs were formed just to have fun. That's not to say that they also educate.

Meet and Eat Club

Marge Haider created this Club in June of 2005. The group consists of individuals who enjoy cooking.

The group meets one month to prepare the menu. All members of the group agree to make something and bring it to the meal the following month. Group leader, Marge, gathers the cooks and all make the decision as to the kind of meal they will have.

The following month the group brings their individual dishes that they have prepared and sit down to a meal. The group has celebrated holidays with special dishes or has had a special kind of meal day such as a Stew Day. Meals are followed by conversation, games, or watching movies for a real social event. Occasionally, the group goes to various restaurants in the area for special dining out days.

Meet and Eat Members: Left to Right. Seated. Colleen Hein, Alyce Klarkowski, Ann Maas, Charlene Kikkert, Les Thiede, Jo Thiede, Marion Radtke. Standing (Left to Right) Shirley Henke, Kay Appenfeldt, Shirley Mack, Meet and Eat Coordinator Marge Haider, Annie Nielsen, Terry Appenfeldt, Rena Hughes, Judy Beyer Not pictured Nancy Braatz, Elmer Kikkert, Caroline Patterson, John Haider

The Fishing Club

The Fishing Club started in April of 2005. Dwayne Braun was the charter volunteer coordinator. The group met at different lakes in the area for fishing. They carpooled and shared gas expenses. Of course, all had to have a fishing license.

Current volunteer coordinators, Gerald Wagner and Terry Zimmerlee, bring in informational speakers and coordinate special events and tours of sporting facilities. Discussions occur about how to fish local lakes using the right bait, where fish can be hiding onshore or from a boat, or how to tie knots to attach their favorite bait to the line. Of course, they still fish at their favorite spots together.

Fishing with Residents of Golden Living Center

Eight members of the fishing club and nine Golden Living Center residents shared a day of fishing in June of 2009. Fishing club members helped this special group of older adults to have a great day of fishing at Tahoe Park. Residents are proud to say that they caught walleye, bullheads, carp, white bass, and small black bass.

Kids Fishing Day

Members of the Fishing Club helped the Beaver Dam Lake Improvement Association with a fishing event at Edgewater Park in 2009. Members taught children to fish. Fishing poles are provided and Fishing Club volunteers bait hooks, help a child to use a rod and reel, and show a child how to take a fish from the line. This event is held annually.

The Fishing Club Members: (left to right) Frank Butts, Keith Grotjohn, Marge Haider, Ken Field, Barb Hammer, Volunteer Coordinator Gerald Wagner, Mary Ziebill, Roger Blasé, Gene Beier, Volunteer Coordinator Terry Zimmerlee, Adam Carthen, owner Artic Fisherman Not pictured: Ralph Trejo, Dwayne Braun, Arden (Bud) Fritz, Rip Cullen, Kenneth Eilenfeldt. Deceased: Darwin Bremer, Larry Koeppen, Don Jacob

Charter Fishing

Members participated in a Lake Michigan charter fishing event in August 2009. The group tries to charter a Lake Michigan fishing trip each year. The fishermen that participated were Keith Eilenfeldt, Roger Blasé, Larry Koeppen, and Terry Zimmerlee.

Fish Fry with the Fishing Club and Meet and Eat

The two groups combined in 2005, 2006, 2007, and 2008 for a fish fry. Meet and Eat cooks and Fishing Club cooks prepared a meal with fish caught by the Fishing Club.

Cooks (left) Don Jacob (right) Gerald Wagner

The Meet and Eat group prepared the rest of the meal. At the first fry, 200 plus bluegills, crappies, bullheads, catfish, perch, and pike fillets were prepared.

Fish fryer Shirley Henke

Neither

In 2009, fishing was not as good so the group celebrated with fish at Ponderosa. In 2010, the group met and fish was ordered and eaten at John's Bar.

The food is on the table and the group serves themselves in a potluck style supper.

Wii Bowling League

Mary Morgan started as the volunteer coordinator for this league in January 2009. The Wii is a computer system that uses a remote instead of a bowling ball.

The bowlers attach the remotes to their wrists (so they don't accidentally throw the remote into the TV screen), push the A button on the remote to get on the alley, push the arrow buttons on the remote to position themselves on the alley, push the B button, aim the remote at the screen, toss the remote as in bowling (but leave it in your hand), and release the B button. Whalla, a strike! Scores are totaled just as in bowling. At this time, bowlers participate to see how high a score they can bowl.

Current bowlers are Marsha Horne, Shirley Mack, Bev Nehmer, Marion Radtke, Mary Morgan, Kay Appenfeldt, Ginny Hodgson, Nancy Braatz, Delores Firari, Nancy Schwartz, Rena Hughes, Lorna Schultz, Shirley Rabbitt, Doris Domann, Frank Schliesman, Genny Schanen, Elizabeth Bestor, and Betty Eilbes.

Starting with the bowling season in 2010, a league will be formed. Betty Eilbes and Mary are putting together the season now.

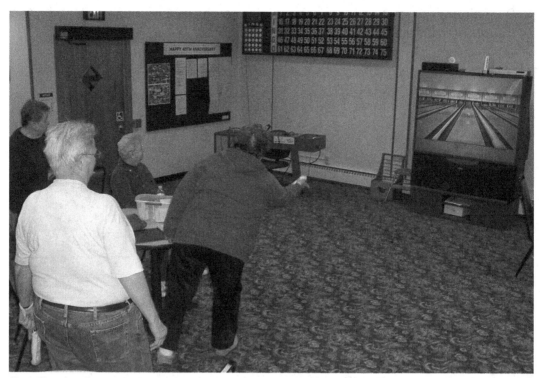

Bowling a Game with Wii. Mary Morgan stands as the Volunteer Coordinator

Of course, we have to remember to have fun and socialize with special events for our light hearted side. The following pages highlight some of these special events.

Polka Party

Who doesn't like to polka? With that thought in mind, the Steering Committee from the Senior Center sponsored a polka party on February 13, 2005. The event was held at the Elks Club. Tony Rechek provided the polka music.

Christmas Parties

2004. Holiday Gala. Entertainment was provided by Dan Sullivan, "Merry Christmas from Me and My Guitar." There was a buffet supper at the Senior Center and the Third Street Band performed.

Having a Good Time at the Christmas Party—2004

<u>2005.</u> Holiday Party. The party was held at Bayside Supper Club. There was a sandwich buffet supper. Music was provided by Randy Kiel the Big Kahuna—One Man Band.

<u>2006.</u> Christmas Party. The party was held at the Beaver Dam Country Club. A buffet and music by Die Spiel Masters provided the tunes for dancing. The Third Street Band performed.

<u>2007.</u> Christmas Party. The Don Peachey Orchestra performed at Bayside Supper Club. A buffet supper and dancing got the people in a holiday mood.

<u>2008.</u> Christmas Party. The party was once again held at Bayside Supper Club. The Third Street Band performed. The Pete Rundy Band provided the dance music. A buffet supper was served. Members were asked to bring a plate of their favorite cookies. The cookies were placed on a serving table. How good those home baked cookies tasted.

<u>2009.</u> Christmas Party. Dante's Bop provided a blend of country, pop, and jazz as the members danced. A family style supper was held at Bayside Supper Club. Members once again brought a plate of their favorite cookies.

<u>2010.</u> Christmas Party. Jeff Hall, a local DJ, provided the music for participants to dance, sit and enjoy the music, or sing along. A family style supper and dessert were served at Bayside Supper Club.

<u>Christmas Gifts.</u> For each of these Christmas parties, the presents were donated by <u>Mabel Schley</u>. See her special story in the Giving Section.

Otis Spunkmeyer Cookies

Speaking of cookies, the Senior Center contracted to bake Otis Spunkmeyer cookies starting in 2007. Del Schultz baked the cookies. Later he was assisted by Gert Miller. Gert has since retired from cookie baking, but Del continues to bake cookies for the Center or for special orders.

The dough is frozen and stored at the Center. Each day the cookies are baked in a special oven. The cookies are S'mores, Carnival (with M & M's) chocolate chip, peanut butter chocolate chunk, turtle and strawberry shortcake. They sell individually, by the threesome, or by the dozen.

They are always a special treat. Frequently, certificates for Otis's cookies are given as door prizes for various events at the Center. They even find their way onto a tour bus occasionally.

The Christmas Parades

Each year since 2002, the Senior Center has had an entry in the Christmas Parade held in December in the city of Beaver Dam. At this event, the Senior Center elves hand out handcrafted Christmas cars from the Senior Center Woodshop to children along the parade route.

Christmas for Critters

What a great name for a Christmas float in 2003. Jim Schwartz, Rich Krahenbuhl, Ron Andrews, Jack Schmidt, and Chuck Yagodinski built this float. It won first prize in its category that evening.

Santa and Mrs. Clause were on the float represented by Oscar Mellenthin and Gloria Klug. Santa's helpers were Marion Radtke, Rich Krahenbuhl, Lynn Winkie, and Deloris Mellenthin.

The Christmas for Critters Float—2003

Gingerbread House

A gingerbread house was the theme for the float in 2004. Those that built the float were Jim Schwartz, Don Jacob, Chuck Yagodinski, Jack Schmidt, Ken Hardinger, and Bill Christian. Sandy Skalitzky helped with the decorations.

Rich Krahenbuhl agreed to be Santa on the float. The float took second place in its category that evening.

Rich Krahenbuhl as Santa on the Gingerbread float-2004

In 2005, the float took third place. In 2006, Terry Appenfeldt drove his truck through the parade. The Christmas cars were in the truck box. Elves had a hard time keeping up with the truck, but all Christmas cars were delivered.

In 2007, a gingerbread house theme reoccurred. Builders Rich Krahenbuhl, Bill Christian, Lewis Terlisner, and Terry Appenfeldt built the float in the Beaver Dam Parks Shop. Windows opened in the gingerbread house and riders Alice Engebretson, John and Marge Haider, and Rena Hughes opened and closed the windows along the parade route. The float took third place.

In 2008, Lewis Terlisner, Rich Krahenbuhl, and Terry Appenfeldt built a car that represented the era of Dillinger for the float. The Beaver Dam Parks Shop provided the space to build the float. The film, <u>Dillinger,</u> starring Johnny Depp had been filmed in Columbus and Beaver Dam during March of 2008. The float modeled the Christmas cars that were designed and built to represent the cars that were driven by Johnny Depp in the movie. A major snowfall caused the elves to tramp through inches and inches of snow to hand out the cars.

The car from the era of Dillinger to honor the film
<u>Dillinger</u> shot in Columbus and Beaver Dam in 2008.

In 2009, Terry Appenfeldt drove his truck through the parade route. In 2010, Louis Terlisner drove his truck to pull the trailer holding the Senior Center lighted display sign. The sign read, "<u>Handcrafted Christmas cars Built by the Senior Center Woodshop.</u>"

Newly remodeled sign showing recognition for the handcrafted
Christmas cars—2010

There were so many children on the parade route in 2009 and 2010 that the elves
ran out of cars to give away. Each was a beautiful winter night—though chilly.

The Christmas That Almost Wasn't

A group of Senior Center actors formed a theatrical group called Senior Thespians in
September 2005. Later in November 2005, they changed their name to Third Street
Players. Their first production was a play called The Christmas That Almost Wasn't.
It was directed by Larry Koeppen. The play was written by K. Gilbreth and modified
by E. Koeppen. The play was performed at the 3 p.m. performance of Bows and
Holly at the Beaver Dam Community Theatre. After their Christmas play, the group
hoped to have a murder mystery or other plays, but it never happened.

The Christmas That Almost Wasn't Cast

The cast included: Santa Claus: John Patterson; Mrs. Claus: Rita Spangler; Dr. Grump (the Villian): Paul Albrecht; Betty Bob, Reindeer Trainer: Betty Eilbes; C.J. Scoop, WXMAS: Nelda Machkovech; Spirit of Christmas: Kayla Jewell; Tanya Tune: Betty Eilbes; Wilma Winner: Judy Jansen; Samantha Smart: Natalie Machkovech; Orville Goodfellow: Larry Koeppen; Viola Vanity: Kelly Warns; Ellie O'Toole: Gloria Wolff; Bonnie Boastful: Marilyn Zamora.

Remembering Senior Center Veterans

Our men and women in service or our veterans were remembered in several ceremonies at the Senior Center in the Recent Years.

Memorial Day Parade

The Senior Center has participated in the Memorial Day Parade to honor veterans from our membership. Dwayne Braun has coordinated the event since 2004.

In that first year (2004), Jim and Loraine Ackley were to ride in the parade representing the Center's acknowledgment of our veterans. Jim was a veteran of World War II. However, the parade was rained out. In 2005, Jim and Loraine were able to be our representatives in the parade.

In 2006, Julian Buss was honored by the Senior Center. Julian was a veteran Marine from the Pacific Theater in World War II.

Julian Buss, World War II veteran and wife in back seat.

In 2008, John Polchinski was honored by the Senior Center. John was in Company D711, a tank batallion in World War II.

John Polchinski, World War II veteran

In 2009, World War II veterans Harvey Schoeffel, Larry Mielke, John Polchinski, Bob Bradley, Del Schultz, and Arden "Bud" Fritz were honored by the Senior Center. All were veterans of World War II.

Harvey Schoeffel, Larry Mielke, John Polchinski World War II veterans

Bob Bradley, Del Schultz, Arden (Bud) Fritz World War II veterans

In 2010, World War II veteran Les Thiede and Vietnam veterans Gerald Wagner and Lewis Terlisner were honored in the Memorial Parade.

Les Thiede, World War II veteran

Gerald Wagner, Lewis Terlisner Vietnam Veterans

Veterans Day

The Senior Center remembers its members who are Veterans in a variety of different ways.

Veterans Day Parade

Reduced rates for this day tour were provided to the Veterans who attended in 2004. On a beautiful fall day in November in Milwaukee, the Veterans and friends and family members had special seats reserved to watch the Veterans Day Parade in Milwaukee. As the parade proceeded, guests ate from boxed lunches. A Veteran's Day memorial occurred at the War Memorial.

Veterans Day Luncheon

In 2005, a complimentary lunch was provided for veterans and was held at the Senior Center. State Senator Scott Fitzgerald was the featured speaker. Veterans' Day greeting cards were sent to 1st Lt. John Koeppen's platoon of the Wisconsin Army National Guard, 128th FA newly stationed in Iraq.

USO Show

A day tour to the Milk Pail Theatre in East Dundee, Illinois, honored the Veterans in 2006. A USO show, remembering the USO tours of old, was presented. Memories of songs of the war years, dances, and stories placed those in attendance in that time in our history and the special music of those times.

High Ground Veterans Memorial Park—2007

A day tour (reduced rates for Veterans) was taken to the High Ground Veterans Memorial Park in Neillsville. A guided tour of the park was provided which honored all veterans from all wars. Especially memorable was the recently built Korean War memorial. A quiet peaceful remembrance was felt in this park totally dedicated to veterans. It was built so veterans would have a place to come to seek solace. A prayer session was held at the end of the tour.

Service Picture Photo Contest

In 2007, seven servicemen placed their service photos on display at the Senior Center. A contest was held to name as many of the servicemen as one could identify. Marsha Horne won the contest by identifying five out of the seven—$25 was the contest prize.

Honor Flight Program—World II Veterans

In 2008, the Honor Flight program for World War II veterans was held at the Senior Center. Combat and non-Combat Military Veterans from all area surrounding American Legions were invited to attend. Mark Grams, County Veterans Service Officer and Dodge County Coordinator of the Honor Flight program, summarized the Honor Flight program. That program flies World War II veterans to the World War II Memorial in Washington, DC.

**BEAVER DAM COMMUNITY ACTIVITIES/
SENIOR CENTER
VETERANS PROGRAM
DECEMBER 4, 2008
9:30 a.m.**

Presentation of the Colors: Beaver Dam American Legion **Post 146** Color Guard

Introduction: **Don Jacob** Staff Sergeant, United States Air Force
Occupational Forces Europe, Berlin, Germany
1946 AACS—50th Fighter Bomber Wing
Past Vice Chair, Beaver Dam Senior Center
Steering Committee

Honor Flight/Guardian Programs: **Mark Grams**, County Veterans Service Officer
United States Marines, Gunnery Sergeant (retired)

Honor Flight Honorees: **LeRoy Klug** (World War II veteran)
Roland Zuelsdorf (World War II veteran)

Monetary Donation **Del Schultz**: Corporal, United States Marines
Honor Flight Program: 1942-46, Scout/Sniper, Pacific Theatre
Vice Chair Beaver Dam Senior Center
Steering Committee

The Wisconsin Veterans **Harvey and Ellie Schoeffel**
Museum "Oral History" Program: **Harvey**: T5 Corporal United States Army
(46-009-070)
1945-1947, Occupation of Germany
Ellie: Treasurer, Beaver Dam Senior Center
Steering Committee

Introduction of World War II Veterans: **John Polchinski**, United States Army
T5 Tank Driver, Company D 711
Tank Battalion, Pacific Theatre

Retirement of the Colors: Beaver Dam American Legion **Post 146** Color Guard

The Honor Flight Veterans Program—December 4, 2008

The Senior Center gave a monetary donation of $500 to the Honor Flight program—that would support one World War II veteran to go on the Honor Flight to Washington, DC. Memorable were the stories of World War II that were given by World War II veterans who volunteered to do so. The program was coordinated by Kay Appenfeldt.

December 4, 2008. Del Schultz (left) Mark Grams (right)
receiving the Check for the Honor Flight

Flag Day 2005—Beaver Dam Elks Lodge

The Elks Lodge from Beaver Dam chose the Beaver Dam Senior Center as the site to host their Flag Day Ceremony on June 14, 2005. Lt. Col. Jan Bauman, R.N. presented a flag to Senior Center Director, Evonne Koeppen. The Rascals and Rockers sang patriotic songs, children and seniors worked together to send cards and letters to servicemen and women, and the Third Street Band performed.

Benefit Dance for Veterans Center

The American Legion, Post 146, of the city of Beaver Dam were constructing a new Veterans Center in 2006. On March 26, 2006, the Senior Center sponsored a fundraising dance. The proceeds from the dance were given to the American Legion for their new Veteran's Center. The Senior Center paid for the expenses of the event. Tony Spangler and the Sunday Nite Line provided the music for the dancers. About 45 people were in attendance.

The Wisconsin Connection—Sales for Veterans Center

Bob Frankenstein, Commander of the American Legion Post in Beaver Dam at that time, was the author of a book called <u>The Wisconsin Connection.</u> It depicted Beaver Dam during World War II as a rendezvous with history.

The Steering Committee of the Senior Center agreed to put his book on sale at the Senior Center in November 2005. The proceeds of the sale of the book went directly to the building fund for the new Veterans Center.

American Flag from AMVETS

During the time of the building of the Veterans Center, the AMVETS met at the Senior Center. The AMVETS were charged no rental fee. As a token of their thanks, the AMVETS presented a flag to the Senior Center Steering Committee in 2006.

Remodeling in the Recent Years

It seemed as though, remodeling was an endeavor through all the 40 years of the Senior Center. This set of years was no exception.

1. <u>2004.</u> <u>Signs for Garden.</u> The Steering Committee authorized the purchase of three signs from Benike Signs. They were placed on the Senior Center Building and in the garden area. <u>Doorways Moved.</u> The East Entrance doorway was moved to install a protected doorway to eliminate the cold coming into the building. The cost was $2565—$1900 was taken from the Vi Schneider donation—the balance was taken from the Senior Center Account.
2. <u>2005.</u> <u>New Carpeting, Valances, Blinds.</u> Don Jacob and Gloria Klug researched new carpeting for the Main Room of the Center. New carpeting was installed in July, and a <u>Dutch door</u> was placed on the office. Total cost was $6843 and was taken from the Vi Schneider donation. A <u>gravel driveway</u> was installed by the gardens in April. <u>Counters and countertops</u> were placed in the Director's office and the office immediately before the Director's office. The offices were repainted. This was finished in August with monies from the Senior Center Account. The cost of no more than $4000 was approved by the Steering Committee, The <u>Pool Room</u> was insulated.
3. <u>2006.</u> <u>Carpeting</u> was placed in the offices at a cost of $251.64. The money came from the Senior Center Account. A <u>kitchen door</u> was installed. The <u>Ladies' bathroom</u> was improved. The <u>Computer Classroom</u> was repainted.
4. <u>2007.</u> Ellie Schoeffel and Don Jacob researched window treatments for the Main Room. The blinds cost $664. The wooden valances were made by Terry Appenfeldt in the Senior Center Woodshop. They were painted by Harvey and Ellie Schoeffel in May and installed by Terry Appenfeldt in that same month. <u>New dining room tables</u> were researched by Del Schultz and purchased in June. Monies came from the WalMart fall cleanup project.

5. <u>2008.</u> <u>Counters and countertops</u> were installed in the Computer Classroom. The Computer Room and Front Offices were rewired and upgraded in February at a cost of $2600.

Don Jacob starts the removal of the carpet

Renaming of the Department and Construction of an Office

In February 2007, the office was built by the East Entryway in the former Game Room to provide space for the Recreation Department of the City of Beaver Dam. The departments of the City were restructured that year. The Recreation Department and Senior Center were joined and housed at the newly named Senior Center/Recreation building. The department was renamed Beaver Dam Community Activities and Services.

Health and Wellness in the Recent Years

Benefit Specialist.

A benefit specialist has been available to Senior Center members since the retirement of Josephine Rake, who handled that position for a multitude of years. Sherry Whitman handled the program in 1992 but at the Juneau office.

In September 2001, a Benefit Specialist began meeting with Senior Center members at the Senior Center. In 2002, the Benefit Specialist was available at the Center the third Tuesday of the month. Connie Schult served as the Benefit Specialist in 2003 meeting the third Tuesday of the month.

Alice Engebretson is the current Benefit Specialist. She meets with senior citizens every Wednesday morning at the Senior Center. She assists them with Senior Care and insurance specific questions.

Alice Engebretson (on the left) Benefit Specialist at the
Beaver Dam Senior Center helps a client

Senior Care and Medicare Part D. Senior Care started in December of 2004. A seminar introducing Medicare Part D was held in August 2005.

Updates to the Senior Center in the Recent Years

Decisions relative to the Beaver Dam Senior Center made changes to the operation, the newsletter, technological improvements, transportation, recognition of members, and the choice to move to a new location.

Spotlight

The Spotlight program began in March 2006 as a suggestion by Kay Appenfeldt, Steering Committee Chair, to recognize Senior Center members for their volunteer activities.

Some of those honored are Marion Gade, Mabel Schley, Don Jacob, Alice Engebretson, Rita Spangler, Gloria Klug, Del Schultz, Peg Slez, Iva Dorn, Rena Hughes, Marion Radtke, Jean Schweitzel, Jim Rollins, Josephine Rake, Rich Krahenbuhl, Kay Appenfeldt, Terry Appenfeldt, Loretta Richter, the Building Committee, Dodge County Nutrition Site, Norm Reier Greenhouse, Third Street Band, Picnics of the Past, Betty Eilbes, Arts and Crafts Instructors, Woodshop, Tour Escorts, Mary Ann Hussli, Ellie Schoeffel, Judy Hill, and Bob Stafford.

One can never measure what it means to volunteer your time to help others, to help the Senior Center, to help your community. This "Spotlight" is just a way to say "Thanks."

New Look for Newsletter in 2008

The Steering Committee approved contracting with LPI, a publishing company, to print the monthly newsletter starting in August 2008. Their representatives came to the Senior Center and called businesses in the area to contract for the advertising within the Newsletter. One thousand copies of the newsletter are produced each month.

Community Center Courier

In December 2008, a new name was sought for the newsletter, Leisure News. Seventy entries were submitted to try to rename the newsletter. The names that were entered were Senior Center Informant, Senior Center Update, The Informant, The Sr. Informant, Senior News in Action, Seniors In Action, The Senior Reporter, Senior Moments, Senior Scoop, Sage Stage Times, Active Aging Monthly, The Silver Bulletin, Senior Lifestyle Newsletter, Busy Beavers, Beaver Action, Senior Rag, Beaver Rag, Community Center Courier, Kaffee Klatch, Break Time, Senior Center Moments, The Senior Dispatch, Keeping Up, Latest Info, Things to Do, Monthly Update, Senior Happenings, Classic Action, Third St. Rag, Elderberry Droppings, Seniors Haven, Geezer Tails, Beaver Blather, Golden Globe, Forward Planner, New Day Activities, The Messenger, Senior Safari, Come Join Us!, Action Center News, Bubbling News, Scoop News, The Senior News, The Senior Center News, Golden Beavers, Golden Age Beavers, Golden Ages, Golden Years, Beaver Dam C.A.N., B.D.C.A.N., Bits and Pieces, What's New To Do, Pulse Beat, The Golden Beavers, The Golden Years, The Senior Chit Chat, The Chatter Box, Elder Seniors, Senior Happenings, The Elder Beavers, The Senior Beavers, The Beaver Happenings, Senior Advisor, Center Digest, Center Insights, Best Years News, Senior Moments, The Flyer, and Center Scoop.

The Steering Committee chose the winner—Community Center Courier submitted by Ellie Schoeffel. The Courier started in January 2009. Ellie stated that her $50 winning prize would be donated to the World War II Honor Flight Program.

The Newsletter Folders

Barb Aplin, Dan Hankes, Audrey Hein, Judy Hill, Rena Hughes, Mary Ann Hussli, Beth Keitzman, Marion Radtke, Audrey Roberts, Audrey Roedl, Betty Rutta, Ellie & Harvey Schoeffel, Elaine Schultz, and Annie Nielsen are on call to fold newsletters monthly. They fold them for distribution to paid subscribers, local businesses, and for the members and guests at the Center.

Senior Center Membership in Professional Organizations/Associations

The Beaver Dam Senior Center and Recreation has memberships in the North American Bluebird Society, Bluebird Restoration Association of Wisconsin, Horicon Marsh Bird Club, Wisconsin Natural Resources, National Association of Senior Centers, National Council on Aging, Beaver Dam Chamber of Commerce, Dodge County Historical Society, Coalition of Wisconsin Aging Groups, Wisconsin Park and Recreation Association, Wisconsin Volunteer Council, the Beaver Dam Chamber of Commerce, and the Wisconsin Association of Senior Centers.

Beaver Dam Senior Center Placed on Cable Channel

In June 2008, the Senior Center and Recreation programs and activities were posted on the City Cable Channel. The current channel number is Channel 994.

Steering Committee Minutes Forwarded to City of Beaver Dam Officials

The Steering Committee minutes were forwarded monthly to the Mayor and Common Council starting in September 2005. The minutes were also posted on the Center's website.

Beaver Dam Senior Center Annual Meeting Date Changed

The Annual Meeting and election of officers to the Steering Committee has been held annually in April since its inception in 1984.

The Bylaw change to hold the elections and Annual meeting in January was recommended by the Steering Committee in January 2006. The Bylaws were approved by the Senior Center membership at the annual meeting. Voting for Steering Committee members were to be held on one day in the third week of January. The Annual meeting was to be held on the last week in January.

Senior Center Nonresident Fees Change in 2007 and 2009

The nonresident fees had not changed since 1976 when the $5 fee was instituted. In December 2007, the Steering Committee recommended raising the nonresident fee to $7. This change was approved at the City level by the Administrative Committee of the Common Council. The Senior Center membership approved the Bylaws at the annual meeting.

In November 2009, the Steering Committee recommended changing the Bylaws to raise the nonresident fees to $10. This change was approved at the City level by the Administrative Committee of the Common Council. The fee was approved by the Senior Center membership at the annual meeting in January 2010.

Subsidized Taxi Rides Changed

Due to the increased cost of subsidizing taxi rides from the City Senior Center budget, a letter was sent to part-time and full-time taxi riders who rode to and from the Center in January of 2005. The letter asked the taxi users to give donations toward taxi transportation. However, this only partly solved the taxi cost ($6000 per year) to the City Senior Center budget. Therefore, in August 2007, a new policy was established by the Steering Committee and put into effect in September 2007. Riders to and from the Beaver Dam Senior Center would pay 50 cents per ride. Riders would also buy a punched card for $5. The card would be good for 10 rides.

Those requiring financial assistance were encouraged to talk with the Administrator—the Administrator or Steering Committee did not want anyone to stop coming to the Center due to the cost.

Beaver Dam Community Activities and Services

TAXI SERVICE POLICY & PROCEDURE—Effective September 1, 2007

Senior Center members can participate in the transportation service to the Senior Center/Recreation facility located at 114 E. Third Street. Two thirds of the cost of this service will be subsidized by the Center. Participants may come to the Center as many times a day as they choose. This service will be extended to special events or activities for the Senior Center held at another location.

Eligibility:
1. Participants must be a registered member of the Senior Center.
2. Participants must be a resident of the City of Beaver Dam.
3. Participants must be 60 years or over for the Senior rate (taxi regulation).

Procedure:
1. Register with the Senior Center to be listed as a passenger.
2. Purchase a punch card at 50 cents per ride (current cost of a Senior ride is $1.50 per trip), 10 punches on a card, $5.00.
3. Each time a ride is taken, the taxi driver will punch the card.
4. Riders are responsible for their cards, lost cards cannot be replaced, and there is no expiration date.

5. Financial assistance will be available for those who find this a hardship. Passengers will meet with the Administrator to make this request.

<u>Senior Center Bylaw Changes 2009</u>

In 2009, the Steering Committee recommended the Bylaw change to hold the Steering Committee elections over a one-week period in the third week of January. A fifth standing committee was also recommended—that fifth standing committee was an Archives Committee. The Senior Center membership approved the Bylaw changes at the annual meeting.

<u>Archives Committee</u>

The Archives Committee was added as the fifth Standing Committee of the Steering Committee in 2009. The Archives Committee is responsible for preserving all the records of the Senior Center.

<u>Senior Center Bylaw Changes to Steering Committee Membership in 2010</u>

The Bylaw changes included a change to the membership of the Steering Committee. The changes stated that the Committee would consist of 12 voting members and the Administrator. Eight voting members are active Senior Center members and are elected by the membership. Three Committee members with the ability to vote shall be selected from the public-at-large by a Nominations Committee (a Standing Committee of the Steering Committee). One voting Committee member would be appointed by the Mayor to serve as a liaison between the Common Council and the Steering Committee.

<u>Code of Conduct</u>

A Section was added to Article IV—Steering Committee of the Bylaws which implements a Code of Conduct to include a Code of Ethics, Conflict of Interest policy, and Non-Retaliation policy for the Steering Committee membership. Each member of the Steering Committee will sign this Code of Conduct policy.

Theses changes were approved at the City level by the Administrative Committee of the Common Council. The Senior Center membership approved the Bylaw changes at the Annual Meeting.

<u>Nominations Committee</u>

This sixth Standing Committee of the Steering Committee was formed in 2011 for the purpose of establishing the criteria for and nominating three public-at-large members to the Steering Committee. The Committee was given the responsibility of selecting those three members from the community of Beaver Dam.

Common Council Liaisons to the Steering Committee

The Mayor appoints a liaison to the Beaver Dam Senior Center Steering Committee from the Alderpersons of the Common Council. Bill Hollihan served on the Committee from 1997 until 2005. Bob Maly represented the Common Council from 2005 to 2006. Ron Andrews served as liaison from April of 2006 to July of 2008. Aaron Onsrud served the remainder of 2008 until May of 2009. Donna Fuhrman is the current liaison and started in May of 2009.

Chamber of Commerce Membership

The Beaver Dam Senior Center Steering Committee recommended that the Senior Center join the Chamber of Commerce. The Senior Center became a member of the Beaver Dam Chamber of Commerce in November 2005.

Downtown Committee of the Beaver Dam Chamber of Commerce

In 2007, the Steering Committee determined that the Senior Center should be represented at the Downtown Committee of the Chamber of Commerce. The Senior Center is located in the downtown jurisdiction. The Committee met monthly. The Downtown Committee explored various ways to improve the downtown and determined how the downtown could become a renewed viable entity to the city of Beaver Dam.

Gloria Klug served as our first liaison to the Committee. She reported back to the Steering Committee on the Downtown Committee activities under the title of Building Committee. Upon her retirement, Kay Appenfeldt became the liaison. The Downtown Committee dissolved in 2010. Downtown Beaver Dam, Inc. was formed and replaced the Downtown Committee. Officers were elected in March 2010. Kay serves as Secretary and also sits on the Design Committee of Downtown Beaver Dam, Inc.

Leadership Program from Beaver Dam Chamber of Commerce

The Steering Committee approved the monetary expenditure for a senior citizen to participate in this Leadership Program from the Beaver Dam Chamber of Commerce. The cost for a member to participate was $500-$550.

Center participants for the first three years of the program were Cherie Wille, 2008; Ken Herren, 2009; and Ellen Sushak, 2010. All wrote a monthly column in the Community Center Courier relative to their participation in the program.

The program supports training for future leadership in the community of Beaver Dam. Participants learn about Beaver Dam and the surrounding area in day-long sessions which are held once a month. The sessions meet from August to June. Hopefully, training will encourage participants to become leaders in the community.

Senior Center Month

The Administrator of the Senior Center asks the Mayor of Beaver Dam to proclaim September as Senior Center Month. The Mayor recognizes Senior Center Month with a Proclamation. Several Mayors have issued proclamations during their terms of office. The City of Beaver Dam Proclamation on the next page is from Mayor Tom Kennedy, currently Mayor of Beaver Dam.

Kay Appenfeldt

City of Beaver Dam
OFFICE OF THE MAYOR
PROCLAMATION

"SENIOR CENTER MONTH"

Whereas, older Americans are significant members of our society, investing their wisdom and experience to help enrich and better the lives of younger generations; and

Whereas, the Beaver Dam Senior Center has acted as a catalyst for mobilizing the creativity, energy, vitality and commitment of the older residents of the Beaver Dam area; and

Whereas, through the wide array of services, programs and activities, senior centers empower older citizens of the Beaver Dam area to contribute to their own health and well-being and the health and well-being of their fellow citizens of all ages; and

Whereas, the Beaver Dam Senior Center in the City of Beaver Dam affirm the dignity, self worth and independence of older persons by facilitating their decisions and actions; tapping their experiences, skills and knowledge; and enabling their continued contributions to the community;

Now, therefore, as the Mayor of the City of Beaver Dam, Wisconsin, I do hereby proclaim September 2009 as **Senior Center Month** in Beaver Dam and call upon all citizens to recognize the special contributions of the Senior Center participants and the special efforts of the staff and volunteers who work every day to enhance the well-being of the older citizens of our community.

Dated this 4th day of September, 2009.

Thomas A. Kennedy, Mayor
City of Beaver Dam, Wisconsin

Senior Center Month Mayoral Proclamation

Open House 2007

A very successful Open House was held at the Senior Center February 3, 2007. Volunteers manned tables to represent each program or activity at the Center. Each volunteer explained their program. Visitors put their names into paper bags at each program table in order to win the door prizes. Each winner received something appropriate to that program.

People were asked to fill out a survey about what programs they felt were important to the Center. The survey results were used by the Building Committee for their research for a new Community Center/Senior Center site.

Gloria Klug and Alyce Schoenwetter manning a table at the Open House, February 3, 2007

The Steps to a New Facility

Guiding Principles and Goal Statements

The self study for the reaccreditation by the Wisconsin Association of Senior Centers as researched in 2005 and 2006 created Guiding Principles and Goal Statements for ten areas: purpose, governance, community, staff/administration/ volunteers, program, evaluation, finances, records, facility, and reputation. Three or four goals were established for each.

A goal to attract new groups or individuals and increase population at the Center was established under Reputation.

A goal to ensure adequate space for programs/activities for maximum participation and attendance was established under Facility.

It was evident that the current facility needed to be expanded in order to meet the goals created in Facility and Reputation.

Steering Committee Establishes Long-Term Goals

The Steering Committee evaluated the research done for the self study and established long-term goals in June 2006. They were

Year 1: Do a Facility Review and Property Exploration
   a. Recruit volunteer review team
   b. Stage and woodcarving space expansion
Year 2: Finalize Property Decision and Funding
Year 3: Build, Expand, or Move

Facility Review—Remodel Second Floor for Woodshop

Extensive study was assigned to Terry Appenfeldt, Woodshop Coordinator, and his Woodshop team to place the Senior Center Woodshop on the second floor of the Beaver Dam Senior Center. Research began in 2007.

This would free the first floor for additional programming in the space the Woodshop now occupied.

The study took six months. Electricity (the second floor would have its own circuit box), HAV system, heat, air conditioning, lighting, ventilation for a spray booth, fire escape to the roof, a handicap walkway to the second floor, and floor plan with sub flooring were all investigated and approved by Wisconsin Power and Light, the fire chief, and the City inspector. The renovation was estimated to cost a little over $45,000.

The City Park and Recreation Committee, which had jurisdiction over the Senior Center, defeated the project at the Committee level before it even could be presented to the Common Council. The Committee felt it was too much money to invest in a building as a temporary fix.

City Combines Senior Center and Recreation

A reorganization of City services and departments occurred in 2007. In that reorganization, the Recreation Department was combined with the Senior Center.

Beaver Dam Community Activities and Services

The combined Senior Center and Recreation Department was renamed in January of 2007. The new name was Beaver Dam Community Activities and Services. The two departments were housed at the current Beaver Dam Senior Center. The Beaver Dam Senior Center was renamed Beaver Dam Senior Center and Recreation.

Mission Statements

A new mission statement for the Senior Center had been developed with the reaccreditation. The statement reads, **"To promote social, educational, leadership, recreational, and volunteer opportunities for persons aged 50 & over, serving as a community resource on aging."**

The mission statement for Recreation reads, **"Committed to enhancing the quality of life for citizens of all ages of the Beaver Dam area through the promotion, development and maintenance of public recreation and enrichment opportunities, park lands, and park facilities."**

Cramped Space

It had been determined by the Steering Committee that the Senior Center was already cramped for space after the self study. A new office was placed in the Game Room to accommodate the needs of Recreation. The Senior Center and Recreation building were now severely crowded, and the Administrator had to invent ways to run existing programs as well as to introduce new programs in this limited space. Knowing that the mission statements for both departments were to be maintained, the Administrator and Steering Committee moved forward with the plans to move to a new locality.

Public Meeting for a New Community Center/Senior Center

The public was invited to a meeting May 9, 2007, to discuss a new Community Center/Senior Center. Those in attendance were able to voice their concerns, and their statements were recorded. The next step involved developing a committee to move forward with the plan.

Building Committee Created

The newly formed Building Committee met on that same evening in May 2007. The original members of the Committee were Kay Appenfeldt who agreed to Chair the

Committee, Marv Gerdes; Aaron Onsrud, Common Council Representative; Gloria Klug; Mary Reak; and Evonne Koeppen, Administrator of Beaver Dam Community Activities and Services.

Survey of Community and Senior Center Members

The Building Committee developed a survey to elicit input from the community and Senior Center membership. These are the questions on that survey.

1. How would you rate the current Senior Center Recreation Building located at 114 East Third Street?
2. Please select which facilities you would like to see in the Senior/Community Center?
3. How would you rate the current programs/services offered by the Senior/ Recreation Center?
4. Please select which programs you would like to see the Senior/Community Center offer?
5. Please circle your age group.

Surveys were placed in the Senior Center newsletter, <u>Leisure News</u>, in October 2007 and were provided to the community at an Open House in February 2008. Senior Center members and the community were urged to complete and return the surveys to the Center. Both sets of surveys were collected and analyzed by the Building Committee.

Survey Results

The facilities wanted were a media/communication room, art and crafts room, private offices, exercise room, card playing room, gardens, walking track, meeting rooms, woodshop, billiards room, warm water pool, and a greenhouse.

The programs wanted were craft workshops, day trips, woodshop, health seminars, entertainment, walking groups, and a daily lunch program.

Meeting with Strategic Planner

After the results were tabulated, the Building Committee planned their next step. They met with Boris Frank, a professional strategic planner, who explained how to develop a strategic plan in March of 2008. The first steps were to develop a mission statement and goals. They were already established upon the completion of the reaccreditation study.

Brainstorming Session for Building Space Needs

The Committee proceeded to develop the space needs for a new building.

The volunteer coordinators of programs at the Senior Center and Steering Committee members met for a brainstorming session March 25, 2008. Using the survey results as a start, those that participated brainstormed their ideas for what program space requirements would be needed for rooms for a new building.

Areas researched were:
1. What is important, what do you want to do.
2. Possible partners to this building.
3. Discussion of space requirements for specific program areas.

Creating the Floor Plan for a New Building

In April 2008, the Building Committee estimated the square footage of each room based on the space needs meeting.

From April 2008 to July 2008, the Building Committee finalized the floor plan. . The first draft occupied over 37,000 square feet. The Building Committee honed the final layout to 25,550 square feet.

City Facilities/Space Needs Report

In October 2008, Marty Sell of MSA presented his final report of the City Facilities and Space Needs to the Common Council. This report researched City facilities and determined which facilities needed improvement. First priority went to the Police Department. Second priority went to the Senior Center. The floor plan as developed by the Building Committee became part of the City Facilities and Space Needs report. The Common Council approved the City Facilities and Space Needs report; and therefore, the floor plan for a new building as developed by the Building Committee.

Tours of Other Senior Centers and Facilities

Throughout 2007 and 2008, the Building Committee and Steering Committee members toured neighboring senior centers and facilities including Centralia Senior Resource Center in Wisconsin Rapids, Hartford Senior Center, Waunakee Senior Center, and Watertown Senior Center. Monroe Senior Center had its own senior specific exercise facility. Evergreens in Oshkosh had a warm water pool and a therapeutic program of water exercising.

Exploration of Available Properties in Beaver Dam

In 2008, the Building Committee explored properties as possible Senior Center/ Community Center sites. Those visited were Get Fit Fitness Center on Hwy 33, former YMCA on Park Avenue, Pic & Save on Spring Street, Herbergers located at Heritage Village Mall, WMFB building site on Dodge Drive, Fullertons on South Center Street, Metalfab on Madison Street, and DPW/Parks shop on South Street.

After each tour, the Building Committee documented the pros and cons of the site visited.

Summary to Operations Committee of Common Council

In January of 2009, the Building Committee met with the Common Council members of the Operations Committee. A PowerPoint presentation outlined the history of the Senior Center from its inception in 1970, explained the accreditation results and their impact on seeking a new facility, explained why a new facility was needed, and outlined the senior centers visited and city properties explored. The Building Committee asked for approval to proceed with a formalized strategic plan to procure a new building to house the Senior Center and Recreation programs.

Decision Analysis Process

A formal decision analysis process completed by the Building Committee in February and March of 2009 determined the "must and wants" for a new building.

Musts: ADA compliant (elevator if two floors); 25,000 square feet or more (existing structure must accommodate designed floor plan); 140 parking spaces; 3-acre lot; has City leadership approval.

Wants: Meets WASC criteria (near senior housing and services, within walking distance or near public transportation); supported by City leaders; align with City Space Needs Study and Comprehensive Plan; minimize the sum of initial investment, present value and future operating costs for 20 years; convenience of utility hookups; overflow parking; attractive building; occupy by 2011; green operation; green space, walking, gardens; low crime, safety concerns; revenue source (rentals); 4-5 acres for expansion.

The Building Committee applied the decision analysis criteria to the sites that had been toured in the city of Beaver Dam. Each site was rated on a 1 to 10 scale with 10 being the highest. Each facility had to meet the "musts" criteria. A preliminary decision analysis gave the WMFB property and the former Herbergers Department store the highest marks. Both were moved forward as possible sites for the new Senior Center/Community Center.

A Design Firm is Hired

The Building Committee interviewed four design firms. Renschler/Verbicher was chosen by the Building Committee in June of 2009. The design firm gave the committee site planning, opinion of probable cost, project funding assistance, and preliminary designs for both properties. The Building Committee held multiple meetings with the design firm through 2009 to give their input as to the final design of the two sites that were chosen.

Building is Selected

Renschler/Verbicher's contract required the Building Committee to make a decision to move forward with only one of the properties. In September 2009, the Building Committee selected Herbergers as their recommendation for the new Senior Center/Community Center. After an exhaustive four-hour meeting with each Building Committee member using the decision analysis criteria and awarding points, Herbergers had been awarded the most total points by a narrow margin. Since the decision was almost deadlocked, the Chair asked the Administrator to make the decision about the site of the new building.

The Administrator spent the next week meeting with the Mayor and City officials about the Herbergers decision and with the Senior Center and Recreation staff. The Administrator conveyed the results of her research at the next Building Committee meeting and recommended Herbergers. Based on the points of the Decision Analysis process and the input from the Administrator, the Committee moved forward with the Herbergers site.

Common Council Meeting

Evonne Koeppen, Administrator, met at the regularly called meeting of the Common Council in October 2009. She informed the Council that the Building Committee was making the recommendation to move forward with the Herbergers Department store as the future site of the Senior Center/Community Center.

Community Center Ad-Hoc Planning Committee

Mayor Tom Kennedy appointed a Community Center Ad-Hoc Planning Committee in November 2009. The Committee members appointed were President of Common Council, Jon Litscher; Alderperson and Chair of the Administrative Committee, Don Neuert; Alderperson and Chair of the Operations Committee, Laine Meyer; Evonne Koeppen, Beaver Dam Community Services and Activities Administrator; and Kay Appenfeldt, Chair of the Beaver Dam Senior Center Building Committee. Committee advisors were Mayor Tom Kennedy, City Attorney Maryann Schacht, and Director of Administration, John Somers.

The first committee meeting met on November 11, 2009. Committee purposes included becoming informed of the efforts of the Building Committee, learning about Building Committee recommendations for a new facility, visualizing a new Center for the City of Beaver Dam, and engaging members of the Common Council in decisions that needed to be made in regard to a new or renovated building.

Design Plans for Herbergers Arrive for Steering Committee Annual Meeting

The plans for the interior and exterior layout of the Herbergers site arrived at 7:30 on the morning of the Steering Committee annual meeting in January 2010. The designs had been based on input from the Building Committee. The plans were presented to the Senior Center membership.

Evolution of Senior Centers

The Wisconsin Association of Senior Centers issued a history of the evolution of Senior Centers at their annual conference in 2007. The movement to initialize senior centers for the senior population began in the 1970s. Funding from Title III Older Americans Act at the Federal level provided monies to make Senior Centers a reality.

Senior Centers started as places where seniors met socially and participated in social activities. At our Center in 1970, our Senior Center members played cards and bingo, participated in potluck dinners, and visited other Senior Centers which established those social contacts.

Centers evolved as Service Centers in the 1970s and 1980s. Our Senior Center began providing services such as the Dodge County meal site in 1977, blood pressure screenings, health related seminars, and the establishment of the Greenhouse and Woodshop in 1973 and 1974 respectively.

The Beaver Dam Senior Center continues as a place for social activities and services continue to be offered.

However beginning in the 1990s, a new type of Center began its evolution. Centers today serve as Community Centers/Senior Centers where collaborative efforts between multiple sources are shared at the Community Center/Senior Center site.

Moving Toward a Community Center/Senior Center Site

As our Senior Center has always been progressive, the Building Committee welcomed this evolution to this new generation of Community Centers/Senior Centers. The Committee recognized that our Center was ready to move to the next era to which Centers have evolved. The Committee recognized that the Center was in a position to become collaborative partners with other organizations, schools, hospital, health care agencies, or others to become a real partner in the community.

The Building Committee's futuristic thinking included a multi-purpose room and lounge that could be used separately or expanded to accommodate 400 people. A classroom could be divided into four rooms to house four classrooms or four meeting rooms. A conference room would provide additional meeting space. The Building Committee recognized that the rooms would be used for our programming but when not in use for Center programming, the rooms could be used/rented by the community for community events.

The Building Committee wanted to accomplish its mission of becoming a "neighborhood for the community." The Center could do so by using the hallway in front of Herbergers in addition to the great room in the interior of the building to sponsor large group activities for the community such as the cream cheese competition, Senior Expo, and a multitude of other community events. The vision perceived volunteers from the Community Center/Senior Center serving as volunteer coordinators at these events.

The Building Committee visualized that a sound studio would house the City's cable channel with a volunteer(s) to keep the City's cable channel updated. Center volunteers could also provide training for area children, residents, as well as seniors in various programs/activities initializing multiple collaborative opportunities in the rooms in the new Center.

The floor plan allowed for separate Senior Center and Community Center areas. The floor plan allowed for the Senior Center area to be sealed during community events so the community would have their own space much like the Waunakee Senior Center. The Building Committee recognized that a separate Senior Center space would meet the requirements for applying for the Community Development Block Grant ($500,000 to $750,000) to help offset the renovation costs for the building. The larger rooms provided space for current programming and additional space for new and innovative programming for seniors.

Being community minded, the Building Committee perceived that the Community Center/Senior Center could revitalize the mall which modeled the plan used for the Centralia Senior Resource Center in Wisconsin Rapids. Lastly, the Building Committee perceived that housing the Community Center/Senior Center at Herbergers would possibly energize business to re-emerge at the Heritage Village Mall.

Renschler Verbicher Presentation to Ad-Hoc Committee

On January 13, 2010, Renschler/Verbicher presented the floor and site plans for the Herbergers site to the Ad-Hoc Committee of the Common Council and discussed funding sources.

The Ad-Hoc Committee at its January 13 meeting stated that the Building Committee could move forward to seek funding from the community through a funding feasibility study.

Funding Feasibility Firm Hired

After interviewing three candidates, the Building Committee selected the McDonald Schaefer Group to conduct the feasibility study beginning in February and continuing throughout the spring of 2010.

The Building Committee: Seated (left to right) Larry Neitzel, Ellie Schoeffel, Don Jacob, Mary Ann Hussli, Marv Gerdes, Ellen Sushak, Ken Herren, Kay Appenfeldt, Chair. Standing: Terry Appenfeldt Not pictured: Darrell Kalmes, Traci Gmeinder, Evonne Koeppen, Terry Zimmerlee

Funding Feasibility Results

Mary McCann of McDonald Schaefer Group presented the Executive Summary highlighting the results of the feasibility study in July of 2010. Both the Building Committee and the Community Center ad Hoc Planning Committee of the Common Council were informed,

The Group tested three areas:
1. Impressions of the Community Activities and Services Department including the Senior Center;
2. Impression of the Plan to purchase and renovate the Herberger's Department Store for the new Community Center/Senior Center.
3. The feasibility of raising $4.5 million to purchase and renovate Herberger's.

The Community Activities and Services Department including the Senior Center are regarded highly in the community. Those interviewed know that the Center offers a wide range of programming for all ages.

Those interviewed recognized that there isn't room for expansion at the current Center and there is a lack of space for existing programming and any future programming.

The proposed plan to purchase and renovate Herberger's showed 44% of the respondents were in favor of the plan, 28% were neutral, and 28% were opposed to the plan.

The Group determined that the $4.5 million was more than could be raised at that time. It was determined that an achievable goal would be $500,000 to $750,000 range. Additionally, the Department of Commerce Community Block Development Grant would offer another $500,000 raising the amount able to be raised as $1 million to $1.2 million.

The complete Capital Campaign Feasibility Study Report is housed in the Archives of the Beaver Dam Senior Center.

Community Center ad Hoc Planning Committee of the Common Council

After the presentation by Mary McCann from McDonald Schaefer Group on September 8, 2010, the ad Hoc Committee concurred that the money able to be raised was not enough to proceed with the project.

The Committee concurred that the people who worked on this project (Kay Appenfeldt and the Building Committee) had been very dedicated and had donated hundreds of hours of time.

The Committee thought that other sites should be explored, and the project should not be dropped. The Committee concurred that the recommendation of the site should come from the seniors themselves—that this was not a decision that the ad Hoc Committee should make.

The Committee noted positives from the study.
1. There is interest in a community center.
2. There is an element of fundraising that can be accomplished.
3. There is knowledge that the senior population is growing.
4. This growing population is interested in more programs and space.
5. The senior population is a critical element of the City's multigenerational needs—those needs have not diminished.

A motion was made to have Kay and the Building Committee review the options for sites and bring them back to the ad Hoc Committee when the information is ready.

The Second Phase in the Search for a New Building

Mayor Tom Kennedy met with the Building Committee and a room full of interested senior citizens at the Senior Center/Recreation Building on October 6, 2010. He informed the group that the project for a new Community Center/Senior Center would move forward. Alderperson Donna Fuhrman and Mayor Tom Kennedy joined the Building Committee that evening. A PowerPoint presentation offered two possible sites for the new building: Fullerton's on South Center Street and the Warmka Warehouse on Dodge Drive.

Throughout the months of November 2010 through February 2011, the Building Committee toured sites for the future Community Center/Senior Center. Those sites toured were: Animart Warehouse on Green Valley Road, Beaver Gunite on Mackie Street, Get Fit Health Center on Hwy 33, Fullerton's on South Center Street, vacant land next to the YMCA on Corporate Drive, and the Warmka Warehouse on Dodge Street.

The Committee formed Pros and Cons of each site. Each building was inspected by the Beaver Dam Fire Department and by the City of Beaver Dam Inspection Services and reports were generated by both agencies.

Site Selection Analysis

On January 12, 2011, the Administrator of the Beaver Dam Senior Center/Recreation Building, Evonne Koeppen, and the Building Committee Chair, Kay Appenfeldt, presented the six options as stated in the previous paragraph for the site of the Community Center/Senior Center to the Community Center ad Hoc Committee of the Common Council.

A history of the Senior Center was presented to reflect how the Center has evolved from a place of socialization, to a place offering services such as the Dodge County Meal Site, to its future evolution as place for collaborative partnerships with other community organizations. While social and service activities would continue, the Center's involvement in collaborations was already evident in its membership in Downtown Beaver Dam Inc., Leadership Beaver Dam, and other collaborative activities. The Center has been accredited twice by the Wisconsin Association of Senior Centers and National Accreditation was being sought.

Evonne Koeppen further advised the Committee that a consultant would be hired to do a Site Selection Analysis. The firm hired was MSA from Beaver Dam. The payment of the firm was paid from the Center's endowment fund. Site analysis would be done for the Fullerton's site and the Warmka Warehouse site.

Later, Animart was included in the site analysis. Animart paid for the costs of the site analysis.

Mayor Kennedy advised the Committee that a Business/Facility Plan would be prepared by the Evonne Koeppen, Kay Appenfeldt, and the Building Committee.

Site Selection Analysis Executive Summary

Marty Sell of MSA presented the Executive Summary of the Site Selection Analysis to the Community Center ad Hoc Committee of the Common Council and to the Building Committee in March of 2011.

The plan provided detailed information about each property. After the analysis, Marty recommended that the Fullerton's property be chosen as the future site of the Community Center/Senior Center. It was recommended that the building be expanded to 25,000 square feet. Concern was expressed about parking. Marty noted that the lot would accommodate 75 to 80 cars. Other adjacent City lots could be used for long-term parking especially when tour groups leave the Center.

Facility Plan for the City of Beaver Dam Community and Senior Center

Based on the guidance of Mayor Tom Kennedy, a facility plan was completed by Evonne Koeppen, Administrator, and Kay Appenfeldt, Building Committee Chair, to present to the members of the Common Council, the City Attorney, the Director of Administration, and owners of the sites explored. The Building Committee reviewed the publication before it was disbursed.

The Plan included the following sections: Introduction/Summary, Vision Statement/History, Building Committee Agendas/Minutes, Current Space/Floor Plan, Beaver Dam Community Services and Activities (Senior Center and Recreation) Programs, Building Sites Considered in Alphabetical Order, Financing, Collaborative Partnerships, MSA Site Selection Analysis Report, and Recommendation for the Future Site of the Community Center/Senior Center.

The analysis of each site (Animart, Beaver Gunite, Fullerton's, Get Fit, Warmka, and the vacant land on Corporate Drive) included reports by City Inspection Services and the Fire Department, Pros/Cons of each site as established by the Building Committee, Dodge County Land Records, Tax Parcel Records, City of Beaver Dam Section Maps, and Assessed Value, Acreage, and Zoning Requirements.

Collaborative partnerships were identified with 30 different service organizations for the Senior Center. Working in collaborative partnerships with community organizations in a new Community Center/Senior Center with expanded space it was determined would achieve new and innovative programming for a new generation of seniors or provide expanded multigenerational programming. Additional collaborative programming for recreational programming numbered 14 that were already in place.

The Plan identified the programming for the Senior Center and the programming for Recreation that were currently being offered at the Beaver Dam Senior Center/Recreation Building at East Third Street. Close to 100 programs encompass these two departments under the umbrella of Community Activities and Services. A Space and Program Comparison Chart prepared by Evonne Koeppen listed the square footage needs and program offerings needed in each room in a new facility.

The Report also encompassed the Site Selection Analysis as prepared by MSA. The Plan was hand delivered to the Common Council on March 25, 2011.

Vision Statement for a New Facility

The Building Committee approved the following vision statement for the new Community Center/Senior Center.

"A place where Beaver Dam area residents come together for wholesome activities as a "neighborhood for the community."

Building Project Survey

In February 2011, the membership of the Senior Center was asked to complete a survey regarding the new site for the Beaver Dam Community Center/Senior Center.

The following questions were asked: How frequently do you attend the Center? Which activities do you attend? Which site do you prefer for a new facility? Do you require handicap accessibility and transportation? What spaces/rooms do you require at the Center?

The result of the survey questions were included in the Facility Plan for the City of Beaver Dam Community and Senior Center and are on file in the Archives of the Center.

The membership chose Fullerton's as the first choice for the new Center by a margin of four votes. The Warmka Warehouse site had the second highest amount of votes.

Community Center/Senior Center Site is Donated

In a letter dated January 8, 2011, Charley and Gail Fakes expressed their consideration of donating the Fullerton's property to the City as the site for use as the Senior Center. They expressed that seniors are a passion of theirs and would do all that they could to make this happen.

Presentation of the Facility Plan

Evonne Koeppen and Kay Appenfeldt presented a PowerPoint of the Facility Plan to the Community Center ad Hoc Planning Committee on April 6, 2011. The Building Committee was in attendance as well as a room full of interested members of the Beaver Dam Senior Center.

Building Committee Recommends Accepting Fullerton Site

The presentation included the Building Committee's recommendation to accept the Fullerton donation as the future site of the new Community Center/Senior Center.

The Building Committee concurred that the site at the downtown location by the river was excellent. Being community minded, the Committee recognized that this building could be a catalyst to encouraging businesses to locate downtown. Outdoor opportunities could be developed on the river site as a positive locality for the citizens of Beaver Dam. The Building Committee's plan to host community activities can still be realized at this locality, but it was felt that it would require the construction of a total space of 25,000 square feet to accommodate all of the spaces needed to make the Center successful.

The Building Committee recognized the generosity of Charley and Gail Fakes with the donation of the property for the Community Center/Senior Center. Their dedication to the senior population in Beaver Dam was commended by the members of the Committee.

Presentation to Administrative and Operations Committees of the Common Council

The Facility Plan was presented to the Committees on April 11, 2011. Marty Sell presented the Site Selection Analysis Report. The Committees unanimously approved moving the plan forward to the Planning Commission of the City of Beaver Dam.

Planning Commission Meeting

The Planning Commission met on Wednesday, April 27, 2011. The members unanimously approved moving forward with the plan to house the new Community Center/Senior Center at Fullerton's.

Common Council Meetings to Accept the Fullerton Site

On Monday, May 2, 2011, Resolution No. 74-2011 came before the Common Council. The Resolution was to approve entering into an agreement for a proposed gift to the City of Beaver Dam by Jaystone Properties LLC for the vacant former Fullerton Lumber Property Located at 209 South Center Street. The resolution was unanimously approved by all members of the Common Council.

The City Attorney, Mayor, and City officials began the negotiation process to accept the property throughout the months of May and June 2011.

On Monday, June 6, 2011, Resolution No. 96-2011 came before the Common Council. The Resolution authorized the offer of the gift of the real estate at 209 S. Center Street from Jaystone Properties LLC by its only members Charley and Gail Fakes to be hereby approved and appropriate City officials are authorized to execute the same on behalf of the City of Beaver Dam. The resolution was unanimously approved by all members of the Common Council.

<u>Closing on the Fullerton Property and the Keys Accepted</u>

On July 22, 2011, in a formal ceremony at Schacht and Schacht Law Offices the papers were signed formally transferring the property at 209 S. Center Street to the City of Beaver Dam. Those in attendance were: Charley and Gail Fakes, City Attorney Maryann Schacht, Attorney Dave Schacht, Mayor Tom Kennedy, and Administrator Evonne Koeppen.

Closing on the Fullerton Property. Seated (left to right) Gail Fakes; City Attorney, Maryann Schacht; Charley Fakes. Standing (left to right) Attorney Dave Schacht, Mayor Tom Kennedy, Attorney Eric Becker, Adminstrator Evonne Koeppen—It is ironic that Attorney Dave Schacht also closed on the property for the Senior Center at 114 E. Third Street.

An Open House followed at the Fullerton property at 209 S. Center where the keys to the building were given to Evonne Koeppen, Administrator. The Building Committee was in attendance as well as a room full of excited members of the Beaver Dam Senior Center.

Older citizens of the Center, Marion Radtke, Rita Spangler, and Mabel Schley were interviewed for the <u>Daily Citizen</u>, the local paper whose reporter was in attendance. Rita said," I'm glad. I have been very eager for this to happen." Marion said, "I'm happy that I have lived long enough to see this happen." Mabel said, "I enjoy the Senior Center very much. I think this is the nicest spot. It's centralized and very convenient. I'm glad they got this place."

The group that celebrated at the open house for the closing on the property for the new Community Center/Senior Center at 209 S. Center St.
Left to Right (seated) (left to right) Larry Neitzel, Bob Bradley, Alice Harvey, Gail Fakes, Charley Fakes, Mabel Schley, Marion Radtke, City Attorney Maryann Schacht. Standing second row (left to right) Kay Appenfeldt, Administrator Evonne Koeppen, Alice Engebretson, Shirley Neitzel, Alderperson Donna Fuhrman, Rita Spangler, Diane Kalmes, Marty Megale, Barb Hunt, Dot Schultz, Mary Desjarlais, Irene Bell, Dan Baulch, Mayor Tom Kennedy, Ellie Schoeffel. Standing third row (left to right) Darrell Kalmes, Gerald Wagner, Robert Horne, Lorna Schultz, Terry Appenfeldt, Wayne Schmitz, Paul King, Elaine Koehn, Del Schultz, Bev Carlson, Jack Ulrich, Audrey Bartell, Peg Slez, Ellen Sushak

Community Services/Senior Center Planning Group

Mayor Tom Kennedy appointed this Planning Group to formulate a master plan for the property at 209 S. Center Street. Members included Mayor Tom Kennedy, Chair; Evonne Koeppen, Administrator, BDCAS; Kay Appenfeldt, Chair Building Committee;

Ellen Sushak, President, FRIENDS of the Beaver Dam Community Center. Advisors were John Sommers, Director of Administration; Ritchie Piltz, City Engineering Coordinator; and Maryann Schacht, City Attorney.

MSA was hired as the professional consultant. Marty Sell serves as the architect/ consultant for the project. The Committee's first meeting was in August 2011.

Penny Drive—The First Million

The "First Million" Dollar Penny Drive was developed in January 2009. The goal was to collect one million pennies ($10,000) to be used toward the new building. Donations are tracked by weight and a prize will be given to the one who has donated the most pennies by weight at the end of the drive. An expert coin collector goes through the pennies to find those that are valuable. Those are made available for sale to coin collectors.

FRIENDS of the Beaver Dam Community Center

FRIENDS is an unincorporated nonprofit association formed in February 2009. Its purpose is to promote and financially support the current and future development of the Beaver Dam Community Center. That support can be through the acquisition of or maintenance of a new site for the Community Center, for the enhancement and expansion of resources, services, and recreation for senior citizens, and the sponsorship of youth and adult sports and enrichment programs.

The officers for the organization are President, Ellen Sushak; Vice President, Peg Slez; Secretary, Kay Appenfeldt; Treasurer, Del Schultz; Database Manager, Darrell Kalmes. Evonne Koeppen, Administrator, serves as an Advisor to the Association. With the resignation of Del Schultz, Harvey Schoeffel assumed the Treasurer position; and upon his resignation, Wayne Schmitz has assumed the Treasurer responsibility in the second year of the Association.

Membership in the FRIENDS group is by Member, Special Member, Honored Member, Life Member, Distinguished Member, and Business Member. Each membership requires a different monetary contribution.

FRIENDS Representation for the New Building at 209 S. Center Street

The Governing Committee at its monthly meeting on January 10, 2011, approved the following motions
1. Contributions to the capital campaign should not be construed as membership donations,
2. FRIENDS will serve as a repository for the funds collected from the capital campaign for the new facility.
3. FRIENDS would manage the capital campaign.

All three motions were unanimously approved.

Language was written to change the FRIENDS Bylaws regarding funds raised or donated solely for the purpose of purchasing, renovating, and/or building a new community center/senior center. The FRIENDS membership approved the Bylaw amendment at the May 5, 2011, meeting.

Ellen Sushak, President, spoke to the Administrative Committee of the Common Council on May 16, 2011. The Committee was advised that FRIENDS had formed a Building Account and would accept donations and capital campaign monies in that account.

In July, FRIENDS agreed to retain Sauterbak and Associates a professional fundraising consultant to manage the capital campaign for the new Community Center/Senior Center.

Kurt Sauterbak, President of Sauterbak and Associates, began the first stages of the capital campaign in August 2011. His fees will be paid from the Building Fund of FRIENDS, the Center Endowment fund, and from monies raised in the capital campaign.

Coffee, Conversation, and the BS Table

The history would not be complete without mentioning the discussions held at the gathering table at the Senior Center. Stories are exaggerated, discussions about the community are hashed over, friends are remembered, tales of Senior Center happenings are weighed, and decisions whether for the good or bad are made. The Center Director/Administrator can be expected to stop by and coffee is shared by everyone.

The table serves many purposes such as housing sign in sheets for door prizes, registration forms for special events/programs, food for potlucks, and name tags for the guests on the tour bus for a trip day. The table was purchased by Theresa Bellone, Center Director, sometime between 1976 and 1982. It's just a "good 'ole" table" for just about everything.

The Morning Group at the Conversation Table: Jim Rollins, Gerald Wagner, Darrell Kalmes, Rich Krahenbuhl, Ken Hardinger, Wayne Gibbs, Terry Appenfeldt, Lewis Terlisner

The lunch crowd arrives between 10:30 and 11:00. They, too, gather round the table for conversations of the day's events, to share a joke or two, to play games, or to talk about the day's lunch. The table welcomes everyone.

The Lunch Group at the Conversation Table: Sharon Kane, Rose Newman, Lorna Schultz, Darlene Hein, Sandy Skalitsky

The 40th Anniversary Celebration

A 40th Anniversary Committee was formed in September 2008 with Don Jacob as Chair. When Don retired from the Committee, the Archives Committee, a standing committee of the Steering Committee of the Beaver Dam Senior Center, formed a subcommittee to plan the events of the 40th Anniversary Celebration. An activity spotlighting the programs and activities of the Senior Center was planned for each month beginning in May 2009.

This is the schedule of events that were planned by Kay Appenfeldt, Ellie Schoeffel, Jean Schweisthal, Marion Gade, Marion Radtke, Rita Spangler, and Evonne Koeppen, Administrator.

The 40th Anniversary Committee: Seated (left to right) Ellie Schoeffel, Jean Schweisthal, Rita Spangler, Marion Gade. Standing (left to right) Evonne Koeppen, Administrator; Marion Radtke, Kay Appenfeldt. The 40th Anniversary binder/scrapbook is displayed on the table.

May 12, 2009. The greenhouse was spotlighted with a Garden Party.

June 22, 2009. The strawberry feast and the music of the Senior Center were spotlighted. The Third Street Band performed. Members of the Senior Center were asked to complete a quiz on the history of Beaver Dam. Prizes were awarded for the most questions right.

July 29, 2009. Picnics of the past were honored with a picnic at Swan City Park. The 90-year olds from the Center were the honored guests.

August 2009. No activities were planned.

September 11, 2009. Bowling was spotlighted with a party with the Bowling League at Tower Lanes.

October 14, 2009. Arts and Crafts, the Writer's Group, and speaker Nancy Zeiman from Nancy's Notions were spotlighted.

November 18, 2009. The Senior Center Woodshop was spotlighted. The 40th Anniversary Clock made in the Senior Center Woodshop was unveiled.

December 9, 2009. The Christmas Party was held at Bayside Supper Club.

January 13, 2010. The Travel Show was held to introduce the day tours and extended tours of the Travel Club for 2010. The Tour Guides were spotlighted.

February 20, 2010. The Cherry Tree and Chili Supper were revived. Penny bingo was played. Donations were accepted for the new building.

March 15, 2010. Food for Thought. Programs for the Book Club, Genealogy, Meet and Eat, Arthritis Exercise, and the Cooking Classes were spotlighted. The food was prepared by the Meet and Eat group. Dessert was furnished by the Men's Cooking Class.

April 17, 2010. A Senior Olympics event was held with athletes competing from euchre, sheep head, pool, fishing club, and Wii bowling. Gold, silver, and bronze medals were awarded on April 17.

May 4, 2010. A banquet and program to celebrate the 40th Anniversary of the Center opening its doors was held at Bayside Supper Club. Former Beaver Dam Senior Center Directors returned for the event. Audrey Benike was presented with a plaque to honor her as one of the founders of the Beaver Dam Senior Center and as the first Director of the Senior Center.

May 4, 2010: Former Senior Center Directors: (left to right) Jana Stephens (1996-1999); Theresa Bellone (1976-1982); Audrey Benike (first Senior Center Director 1970-1974); Ann Neumaier (1983-1995); Evonne Koeppen (2002 to present). Not pictured are Miriam Simmons (1974-1976) and Amy Palm (1999-2002)

The 40th Anniversary Wall Hanging

Marion Gade crocheted a commemorative wall hanging to celebrate the 40th Anniversary. It holds a special place on the Senior Center wall by the podium.

The 40th Anniversary Bulletin Board

Don Jacob, Marion Gade, and Ellie Schoeffel made the bulletin board from a piece of pink insulation. They covered the board with blue fabric donated by Nancy's Notions, and it was placed on the wall by the Third Street entry.

Throughout the months of the 40th Anniversary celebration, Ellie Schoeffel and Kay Appenfeldt researched the Archives and changed the material on the board to reflect the history that was celebrated each month.

Kay Appenfeldt (left) and Ellie Schoeffel (right) by the 40th Anniversary Bulletin Board

40th Anniversary Scrapbook

Ellie Schoeffel and Rebecca Schultz prepared a detailed scrapbook of the 40th anniversary events. Their work will forever be displayed in the Center Archives as a remembrance of those special days in 2009 and 2010. The book contains photographs and a detailed account of each anniversary event.

The 40TH Anniversary Clock

It started with a catalog and the glimmer of an idea. What could the woodshop create as a gift for the Beaver Dam Senior Center for the 40th anniversary? The glimmer of an idea turned to reality when Terry Appenfeldt found a wooden clock kit in a catalog. "Why can't we make a grandfather clock," he said? With Evonne Koeppen's approval, the kit was purchased.

Terry donated his time to put the clock kit together and stain the wooden parts. The clock was turned over to Bob Stafford, a clockmaker, who donated his time to put in the timing mechanisms. He donated the weights which make the clock keep time. He stored the clock at his house, without charge, while the structure was being built. Terry approached the woodcarvers to ask them if they would carve fixtures for the clock to represent the various programs at the Center. They said, "Sure." Eight different carvers created the following designs: Carving knife and fishing rod: Jack

Ramey; maples leaves/acorns: Buzz Vanderhei; hammer and saw: Don Jacob; crochet, cards, bowling: Marsha Horne; musical notes, exercise person: Alyce Schoenwetter; two movie projectors: Lloyd Lathrop; bird: Corwin Miller; pots and pans: John Monday. Each donated approximately fifteen hours for each carving. Bob Stafford donated his time to place them in different places on the clock surface and glued them down.

Terry and construction advisers Rich Krahenbuhl, Lewis Terlisner, Darrell Kalmes, and Ken Hardinger planned the grandfather clock structure. Lewis donated his time to trace the 40s from a pattern and cut them out carefully with a scroll saw. They form the feet of the clock.

Terry cut the donated wood for the boards for the framing of the structure on the table saw. Terry coordinated the size of the grandfather clock (top to bottom, side to side) with Bob to make sure the clock would fit. Terry designed the clock frame and built the frame including the hickory pieces. He also created the patterns for the molding for the detail of the clock frame.

Two rosettes were used on each corner. The first rosettes, donated by William Sawejka, were cut out by Terry; and a second rosette that was purchased was nailed and glued inside of the first one.

The entire outside structure was stained by Terry using Bombay mahogany stain. Harold Vanderhei donated the hickory wood which was cut by Terry and Ken for the frame of the clock. Bill Flemming planed the boards and Terry donated the money for the expense. Terry used two coats of sanding sealer and two coats of polyurethane for the hickory on the outside edges of the cabinet. The routered pattern, using a bull nosed router bit, in the hickory frame was done by Terry using a jig which Terry, Rich, Lewis, and Ken created. Terry measured the openings for the glass and installed the glass and fixtures that were purchased from SGO Designer Glass LLC from Madison. Bob Stafford donated his time to install the clock and timing mechanisms. The lights were installed by Terry purchasing them from Rockwell.

The 40th Anniversary Clock

The clock was donated to the Center at a celebration honoring the woodshop for the 40th Anniversary on November 18, 2009. The donated time was proudly given to create a memorable gift to commemorate the 40th Anniversary of the Beaver Dam Senior Center. Those that donated their time were the woodcarvers, the clockmaker, Woodshop Manager, Terry Appenfeldt and the Woodshop guys. Estimated donated hours woodcarvers: 180. Estimated time clockmaker: 80 hours. Estimated time Terry Appenfeldt: 400 hours. Estimated time woodshop guys: 70 hours. Donated materials: Northwoods Craftsmen, Harold Vanderhei, William Sawejka, Bob Stafford, and the Woodcarvers.

Clockmakers: (left to right) Harold Vanderhei, Terry Appenfeldt, Don Jacob, Lewis Terlisner, Bob Stafford, Marsha Horne, Rich Krahenbuhl

Senior Center Anniversary Celebrations

10th Anniversary. The first anniversary celebration occurred on Friday, April 15, 1983. This celebrated the 10th anniversary of the purchase of the Senior Center property. The day was celebrated with slides, memorable material, and entertainment. The history of the Center and interesting activities were enjoyed.

20th Anniversary. The second anniversary celebration occurred on October 1, 1993. Rueben Spielberg made a video of the celebration that day which is housed in the Senior Center Archives.

City leaders and Center charter volunteers presented the history of the Center. Speaker Martin Ruge spoke on "How to Stay Alive Until They Lower the Lid." The Mello Tones provided musical entertainment.

Members were charged a $1.00 ($6.00 was paid from the project account) for birthday cake and refreshments.

25th Anniversary. The third celebration held on March 19, 1998, invited guests to an open house to showcase the remodeled Center.

Ray and Evelyn Langmack's monetary donation received recognition with an engraved plaque. James Yanikowski, Attorney, representing the Langmacks said, "Evelyn and Ray would be pleased because it (the money) is being used by you their friends and acquaintances."

Mayor Tom Olsen said, "I think the seniors themselves have contributed generously to the Center."

Al Tucker, Chair of the Steering Committee, thanked the Steering Committee and the Remodeling Committee for their efforts in the remodeling.

Jana Stephens, Senior Center Director, thanked the contractors for their professionalism. She said, "The Beaver Dam Senior Center is unique. We have facilities, volunteers, and participants like no other senior center I know of." A recognition program, refreshments, and tours of the Center completed the day.

30th Anniversary. The fourth celebration held on the afternoon of May 17, 2003, provided music, fun, and refreshments. An anniversary cake reflected the 30th Anniversary of the Center. Casey Carney and Glen Navis provided the music.

Children who were winners of the WASC (Wisconsin Association of Senior Centers) essay contest read their essays at the event.

The 90-Year Olds

The Beaver Dam Senior Center has had the honor of having 90-year old individuals within their membership. Several have had birthday celebrations at the Center. Hooray for them and hooray for the Senior Center to have them in our presence.

Wally Griesbach and Frieda Anton both celebrated their 90th birthdays at the Center—both were active volunteers at the Center

The following 90—and 90+-year olds participated at a picnic at Swan City Park to celebrate the 40th Anniversary of the Center. Each was 90 or older at the time of the event or would turn 90 in 2011. Some dressed in old time costumes for the day.

Doris Domann

Erwin Hammer

Sylvia Lifke

Roman Marek

Erna Miller

John Polchinski

Marion Radtke

Adelle Rosplock

Mabel Schwandt

Rita Spangler

Those Who Worked at the Beaver Dam Senior Center

November 1975: Mary Girard, Secretary (see earlier pages of the history)

The Directors have had able workers, Center volunteers, and guests who participated in working at the Center. Ann Neumaier, Senior Center Director, operated the office with all volunteer help. Following her resignation in 1995, the following workers assisted the new directors.

1996-1997:   **Cindy Jameson**, Senior Center Assistant

1998:   **Dorothy Cerroni**, Receptionist

1998-2000:   **Chuck Cook**, Custodian

1999-2006:   **Coleen Brenton**, Senior Center Assistant

2000 to present: **George Behling**, Custodian

2001:   **Joanne Hofer**, Senior Center Receptionist

2002-2004:   **Darlene Hein**, Receptionist

2004-2005   **Pearl Dobbratz**, Volunteer Receptionist

2004-2007:   **Cheryl Hall**, Center Clerk

Beaver Dam Community Activities and Services

2007-to Present   **Traci Gmeinder**, Office Administrator

2007 to Present   **Patti Maleck**, Customer Service

2008 to 2010   **Rebecca Schultz**, Clerk

2011 to Present   **Karen Ferstl,** Clerk

A Spanish Hamburger Story. Jack Schmidt prepared the Spanish hamburger for a special party at the Senior Center. He prepared the food one day early and placed it in the Senior Center refrigerator. A private party rented the Senior Center that evening. The party members ate the Spanish hamburger for their party, so there was none available for the special event. Jack came in early that morning and prepared another batch. The private party did pay for the cost of the groceries.

Special Message Feature. In May 2007, the new phone system was installed at the Senior Center and Recreation building with the "leave a message" feature.

Matt Kenseth and the Corvette. Toby Schmitt requested that a Corvette Christmas car (made in the Woodshop) be sent to her newly born grandson. The newborn's Dad works as the crew chief for Matt Kenseth, NASCAR driver. The Woodshop received a thank you card from the team which has been placed in a special folder for the Center Woodshop memories.

Cramped Quarters. After the Christmas parade in 2009, Christmas elves Lewis Terlisner, Kay Appenfeldt, Shirley Mack, and Mary Morgan piled into the back seat of Terry Appenfeldt's truck to ride back to the Senior Center. Shirley sat backwards on the console and the rest stuffed into the back seat. You can imagine how cramped they were with all their winter garb, boots, hats and gloves. Terry and Larry Koeppen occupied the front seat of the truck. All were afraid to open the doors upon their return for fear someone would catapult to the next county.

"Popcorn" Hein. Darlene Hein was called "Popcorn", because she was known to prepare popcorn for the Senior Center members for any event from movies to just plain old fashioned conversation.

The Oscars. Louis Grubich would watch all the entertainment television shows prior to the Oscars. He would point out who the winners should be for the Academy Award presentation and use his research to fill in the Oscar ballot for the Academy Award contest. The Movies program coordinator at the Center hosted the contest each year.

Packer Parties. Center members watched the Packers on the large screen TV for Packer parties in September 2004. Lynn Winkie hosted those first parties.

<u>Off to Stevens Point.</u> Two carloads of Senior Center members drove to Stevens Point to be present when Evonne Koeppen received her Senior Center Director of the Year award from WASC in September 2007. Those attending were Don Jacob, Harvey and Ellie Schoeffel, Terry and Kay Appenfeldt, and Alice Engebretson. The members were sworn to keep the Award a surprise, so Evonne did not know that she was receiving the Award or that members were arriving. The members crept down the hallway to go to the bathroom after their arrival and hoped that Evonne would not choose that same time to meet them there. They peered down the hallway before leaving the restroom and seeing that it was all clear hurried back to the lounge area where they waited secretly for the presentation. A member of WASC escorted the group to the awards ceremony. Evonne was surprised.

<u>A Twisting Experience.</u> John Moser from WBEV/WXRO won the Twist dance contest at the Baby Boomer Sock Hop. When asked his name, he said he was Bill McCullum, his co-partner announcer at the morning radio show at WBEV.

<u>The Weather and the Tall Ships.</u> A tour group boarded the bus and headed on a day trip for the Tall Ships docked in Green Bay. Most quickly toured the tall ships and spent the rest of the day at a nearby pub in the air conditioning because it was so hot. On the return trip home, the air conditioner on the bus did not work. When a tour member was dropped off in Waupun at the end of the tour, the bank temperature gauge in Waupun registered 100 degrees.

<u>Yummy, Yummy Baker</u>. Don Jacob was known to treat members of the Senior Center and Fishing Club with his homemade butterhorns baked with cinnamon. What a yummy, yummy treat from a very special guy.

<u>A Dance with a Cow.</u> Betty Stafford grabbed a cow and danced with it as the Whiskey River Band played a song at the Country-Western dance held in October 2009. One couple sat in the middle of the dance floor all night and enjoyed the Whiskey River Band. Dancers danced around them.

<u>The Library.</u> In August 2004, the Center Library occupied a space in the Main Room. Members could check out a book, read it, and return it using a self registration policy.

<u>Remembering the Green Bay Packers.</u> Sandy Sullivan, author of <u>Green Bay Love Stories,</u> spoke to Senior Center members on Valentine's Day, February 14, 2006. She recounted stories of the first Green Bay Packer championship team.

<u>Ho-Ho Hotline.</u> On Monday through Friday, Senior Center members would make phone calls to children pretending to be Santa Claus or Mrs. Claus. The pretend Santa's and Mrs. Clause's did this at Christmas in 2002 and 2003.

A Special Chair. The Steering Committee approved buying a special chair for Mary Hollihan for the woodshop. She was the hole drilling expert for the Christmas cars, and she needed a special chair to do her work.

A Forgotten Saw. When the 40th Anniversary clock was unveiled, woodcarver Don Jacob pointed out that his carved saw was not on the clock. The search began, the saw was found, and two weeks later Bob Stafford glued it on the clock where it remains today.

I Walk the Line. The story of Johnny and June Cash was told in Oscar winning performances in the movie I Walk the Line. Over 35 people attended the movie program on the day this movie was shown at the Center. Chairs had to be pulled from multiple locations to seat everyone.

Pool Success Almost. John Polchinski sunk the 8-ball on the break in a pool game. What a great feat. Unfortunately, the cue ball also decided to go into a pocket right after the 8-ball. Oh darn!

The Third Street Band Performs. The Third Street Band performed at the Senior Expo in 2004. Rita Spangler performed in a lively costume and Third Street Band members created a performance that entertained those in attendance and lived up to their reputation as being the "musical ambassadors" of the Senior Center.

For the Children. In 2003, the Senior Center Steering Committee approved a donation of $250 for the Children's Radiothon. Evonne Koeppen, Senior Center Director, delivered the check.

(John Kraft on the roof of WBEV Radio with the fish bucket; Evonne Koeppen, Senior Center Director on the ground with the check in the bucket

EVONNE KOEPPEN
2002—to present

Evonne joined the Center in 2002. She previously served as the Executive Director for the Belleville, Exeter & Montrose Senior Citizens Program in Belleville, Wisconsin, for ten years prior to accepting the position in Beaver Dam.

In 2007, Evonne was awarded the <u>Professional of the Year</u> by the Wisconsin Association of Senior Centers.

Evonne showing her plaque as Senior Center Director of the Year

Evonne has a weekly radio broadcast highlighting the activities of the Beaver Dam Senior Center and is a frequent guest on the Community Comment specialized radio show. She writes articles and supervises the publication of the monthly <u>Community Center Courier</u> newsletter.

In additional to regularly scheduled programs and activities, Evonne creates special activities for Senior Center Week, Older Americans Month, National Volunteer

Appreciation Week, Grandparents Day, National Health and Fitness Day, one-day and extended day trips, Veterans Day, and other community events.

Evonne has served on the Board of Directors and as President of WASC (Wisconsin Association of Senior Centers) and attends WASC and NCOA conferences and workshops regularly.

Under Evonne's directorship, the following services have been offered to members: Lifeline Screening, blood pressure readings, Benefit Specialist one day per month, Senior Care volunteer weekly, reduced fee taxi services to and from the Center, Medicare Part B and prescription drug seminars, and flu shot clinics.

Under Evonne's directorship, the Third Street Band was initiated, the Veterans Quilt was created, the City's website and cable channel pages were established, the Right Before Lunch, Charter School, It's Movie Time, and multiple exercise programs were developed. The Christmas cars became part of the Christmas parade, and the Capital Improvement Project endowment fund was established.

The Recreation Department was added to her job description in 2007, and she has successfully managed the Senior Center and Recreation Departments under the new department name Beaver Dam Community Activities and Services. There are five permanent full and part—time staff and over 45 seasonal employees working in the department. Eighty plus volunteers donate 9,000 to 10,000 hours of time annually coordinating programs and activities for the membership and guests to the Senior Center and Recreation building.

APPENDIX A
Commission on Aging Members Senior Advisory Board

Commission on Aging Members—1969

Co-chair:	Nancy Nashban
Co-chair	O. A. Paciotti
3-year terms	Audrey Benike
	Don Nolter
2-year terms	Rev. Elton Moore
	Gertrude Deniger
1-year term	Clarence Arndt
	F. M. Sheafor

Senior Advisory Board—1970

Mrs. Adela Neuman, Mrs. Alfred Backhaus, Mrs. Elsie Dinkel, Mrs. Emma Kenitzer, Mrs. Ella Zimmer, Gilbert Schindel

Commission on Aging Members—1970

Chair:	O. A. Paciotti (Bertha Proctor replaced O. A. Paciotti as Chair in November) (Bertha Proctor resigned as Chair in September 1971)
Center Director:	Audrey Benike
Secretary:	Gertrude Deniger
Other members:	Clarence Arndt, Bertha Proctor, Elsie Dinkel, Ella Zimmer, Emma Kenitzer, Don Nolter (resigned October 1, 1970—replaced by John Auten) Rev. Elton Moore, Adela Neuman, Gilbert Schindel

Senior Advisory Board—1971

George Kurtz, Ed Gergen, Carl Finup, Blanche Frandorf, Adela Neuman, and Center Director, Audrey Benike

Commission on Aging Members—1971

Chair:	Betty Maier
Other members:	Helen Ritsch, Tom Olson, O.A. Paciotti, Evelyn Camenga, John Auten

APPENDIX A
Commission on Aging Members/Senior Advisory Board

Commission on Aging—1972

June 6, 1972: A committee started to evaluate the need for a Senior Center facility. They also discussed and made recommendations for administering the Center.

1972 Committee

President:	Andrew Ollinger
Vice President:	Al Karsteadt
Secretary:	Blanche Guse
Treasurer:	Eva Schmidt
Advisory Board:	Jeannette Heimerl, Ed Gergen, Adela Neuman
	(Worked in conjunction with the Commission on Aging)

APPENDIX A
Standing Committees of the Steering Committee

The <u>Standing Committees of the Steering Committee</u> were initiated to oversee certain program areas of the Center. The Greenhouse and Woodshop have been in existence the longest. The following have been voluntary Chairs.

Archives: <u>Current Chair</u>: Kay Appenfeldt

Greenhouse: Wally Greisbach, Al Schultz, Orville Gutgesell, Arvid Behm, Mary Hollihan, Gloria Klug, Darwin Bremer, Marion Gade <u>Current Chair</u>: Jack Ulrich

Nominations: <u>Current Chair:</u> Kay Appenfeldt

Program.   Marge Kopff, Mitz Raschka, Jean Gutgesell, Gloria Klug, Earl Lange, Mary Ann Hussli <u>Current Chair</u>: Gert Miller

Tour: Mary King, Jean Gutgesell, Gladys Wild, Joan Schreiber, Phyllis Cullen, Ron Andrews, Kay Appenfeldt <u>Current Chair:</u> Wayne Schmitz

Woodshop: Norm Reier, Jason Merritt, Don Kopff, Stan Draheim, Bob Jeske, Al Schultz, Art Wallendal, Rich and Norma Krahenbuhl, Jim Schwartz <u>Current Chair:</u> Terry Appenfeldt

1973

President:	Mrs. Alice Lemke (Committee held office for six months)
Treasurer:	Blanche Frandorf
Project Treasurer:	Marie Merrill
Secretary:	Mrs. Doris Graff (resigned in April—Mrs. Giese became Secretary)

President:	Mrs. Jeannette Heimerl (Committee now has one-year term)
Vice President:	Mr. Ollinger
Treasurer:	Mrs. Jo Merrill
Secretary:	Mrs. Giese

1974

President:	Andrew Ollinger
Vice President:	Al Karsteadt
Secretary:	Viola Lohr
Project Treasurer:	Eva Schmidt
Treasurer:	Polly Rosenmeier

1975

President:	Al Karsteadt
Vice President:	Wally Griesbach
Secretary:	Viola Lohr
Treasurer:	Jeannette Heimerl
Project Treasurer:	Eva Schmidt

1976

President:	Al Karsteadt
Vice President:	Wally Griesbach
Secretary:	Eva Schmidt
Treasurer:	Jeannette Heimerl
Project Treasurer:	Viola Lohr

(Eva Schmidt passed away June 12, 1976—Eleanor Charon became Secretary—she resigned on July 27—Viola Lohr became Secretary until the election)

1977

President:	Wally Griesbach
Vice President:	Jeannette Heimerl
Secretary:	Margaret Braeker
Treasurer:	Viola Lohr

1978

President:	Wally Griesbach
Vice President:	Ray Flanders
Secretary:	Margaret Braeker
Project Treasurer:	Tillie Bornkuski

1979

President:	Al Karsteadt
Vice President:	Jeannette Heimerl
Secretary:	Verna Janz

1980

President:	Jeannette Heimerl
Vice President:	Wally Griesbach
Secretary:	Verna Janz

1981

President:	Jeannette Heimerl
Vice President:	Wally Griesbach
Secretary: Elda	Follansbee

1982

President:	Wally Griesbach
Vice President:	Blanche Sharkey
Secretary:	Elda Follansbee
Project Treasurer:	Emma Khalar

APPENDIX B
Beaver Dam Senior Center Advisory Committee and Steering Committee Officers and Members

<u>1983</u>

President:	Wally Griesbach
Vice President:	Elda Follansbee
Secretary:	Margaret Braeker

<u>1984</u>

President:	Elda Follansbee
Vice President:	Phil Esten
Secretary:	Irene Udell
Project Treasurer:	Viola Lohr
Past President:	Wally Griesbach

<u>1985</u>

President:	Gib Brooks
Vice President:	Viola Lohr
Secretary:	Bea Willihnganz
Project Treasurer:	Josephine Rake

<u>1986</u>

President:	Howard Benz
Vice President:	Viola Lohr
Secretary:	Bea Willihnganz
Treasurer:	Josephine Rake

<u>1987</u>

President:	Howard Benz
Vice President:	Viola Lohr
Secretary:	Sybil White
Treasurer:	Josephine Rake

1988

President:	Viola Lohr
Vice President:	Anne Gartland
Secretary:	Sybil White
Treasurer:	Josephine Rake
Past President:	Howard Benz

1989

President:	Viola Lohr
Vice President:	Anne Gartland
Secretary:	Marion Radtke
Treasurer:	Josephine Rake
Past President:	Howard Benz

1990

President:	Anne Gartland
Vice President:	Frieda Anton
Secretary:	Marion Radtke
Treasurer:	Josephine Rake
Past President:	Viola Lohr
Park & Rec:	Cora Moylan

1991

President:	Anne Gartland
Vice President:	Frieda Anton
Secretary:	Marion Radtke
Treasurer:	Josephine Rake
Past President:	Viola Lohr

1992

President:	Marion Radtke
Vice President:	Orville Gutgesell
Secretary:	Marge Kopff
Treasurer:	Josephine Rake

1993

President:	Marion Radtke
Vice President:	Lorraine Krueger
Secretary:	Marge Kopff
Treasurer:	Mary Reilley

1994

President:	Lorraine Krueger
Vice President:	Al Tucker
Secretary:	Anne Gartland
Treasurer:	Mary Reilley

1995

President:	Al Tucker
Vice President:	Pearl Landmann
Secretary:	Marge Bergeman
Treasurer:	Mary Reilley

1996

No officers listed—five elected to the Committee
Anne Gartland, Al Tucker, Marion Radtke, Josephine Rake, Mabel Schley, Mary Reilley Alderperson: Stan Rechek

1997

President:	Al Tucker
Vice President:	Marion Radtke
Secretary:	Josephine Rake
Treasurer:	Mary Reilley
Member:	Mabel Schley
Alderperson:	Bill Hollihan

1998

President:	Al Tucker	Julian Buss
Vice President:	Marion Radtke	Arlene (Silloway) Christian
Secretary:	Kaye Janisch	Josephine Rake
Treasurer:	Mary Reilley	
Alderperson:	Bill Hollihan	

1999

President:	Al Tucker	Rich Krahenbuhl
Vice President:	Julian Buss	Marion Radtke
Secretary:	Kaye Janisch	Arlene (Silloway) Christian
Treasurer:	Mary Reilley	
Alderperson:	Bill Hollihan	

(Al Tucker resigned in June—Julian Buss became President; Rich Krahenbuhl became Vice President)

2000

Chair:	Kathryn Barbour	Rich Krahenbuhl
Vice Chair:	Arlene (Silloway) Christian	Marion Radtke
Secretary:	Julian Buss	Al Tucker
Treasurer:	Mary Reilley	Ron Andrews
Alderperson:	Bill Hollihan	

2001

Chair:	Ron Andrews	Rich Krahenbuhl
Vice Chair:	Marion Radtke	Arlene (Silloway) Christian
Secretary:	Bob Frankenstein	
Treasurer:	Mary Reilley	
Alderperson:	Bill Hollihan	
Past President:	Kathryn Barbour	

2002

Chair:	Ron Andrews	Mary Hollihan
Vice Chair:	Julian Buss	Rich Krahenbuhl
Secretary:	Marion Radtke	Arlene Silloway
Treasurer:	Mary Reilley	Gloria Klug
Alderperson:	Bill Hollihan	Oscar Mellenthin

(Julian resigned in July—Bob Frankenstein became Vice Chair)

2003

Chair:	Lynn Winkie	Julian Buss
Vice Chair:	Bob Frankenstein	Gloria Klug
Secretary:	Oscar Mellenthin	Mary Hollihan
Treasurer:	Alice Engebretson	Ron Andrews
Alderperson:	Bill Hollihan	

2004

Chair:	Lynn Winkie	Gloria Klug
Vice Chair:	Bob Frankenstein	Don Jacob
Secretary:	Kay Appenfeldt	Earl Lange
Treasurer:	Alice Engebretson	Darwin Bremer
Alderperson:	Bill Hollihan	

(Lynn Winkie resigned and was replaced by Bob Frankenstein; Rita Spangler became the new member on the Committee; Earl Lange became Vice Chair)

2005

Chair:	Kay Appenfeldt	Gloria Klug
Vice Chair:	Don Jacob	Rita Spangler
Secretary:	Dwayne Braun	Darwin Bremer
Treasurer:	Alice Engebretson	Earl Lange
Alderperson:	Bob Maly	

2006

Chair:	Kay Appenfeldt	Dwayne Braun
Vice Chair:	Don Jacob	Gloria Klug
Secretary:	Darwin Bremer	Rita Spangler
Treasurer:	Alice Engebretson	Mary Ann Hussli
Alderperson:	Ron Andrews	

2007

Chair:	Kay Appenfeldt	Rita Spangler
Vice Chair:	Don Jacob	Del Schultz
Secretary:	Judy Hill	Marion Gade
Treasurer:	Ellie Schoeffel	Mary Ann Hussli
Alderperson:	Ron Andrews	

2008

Chair:	Ellen Sushak	Mary Ann Hussli
Vice Chair:	Del Schultz	Terry Appenfeldt
Secretary:	Judy Hill	Marion Gade
Treasurer:	Ellie Schoeffel	Rita Spangler
Alderperson:	Ron Andrews until July—replaced by Aaron Onsrud	
Past President:	Kay Appenfeldt	

2009

Chair:	Del Schultz	Mary Ann Hussli
Vice Chair:	Ellen Sushak	Terry Appenfeldt
Secretary:	Peg Slez	Wayne Schmitz
Treasurer:	Ellie Schoeffel	Darrell Kalmes
Alderperson:	Aaron Onsrud until May—replaced by Donna Fuhrman	

2010

Chair:	Del Schultz	Terry Appenfeldt
Vice Chair:	Ellen Sushak	Darrell Kalmes
Secretary:	Peg Slez	Gert Miller
Treasurer:	Wayne Schmitz	Gerald Wagner
Alderperson:	Donna Fuhrman	

APPENDIX C
Roedl-Jacobs Lumber Yard

The property at 114 E. Third Street as owned by Roedl-Jacobs Lumber Company was leased for the Beaver Dam Senior Citizens Center in 1970 and purchased in 1973.

The property consisted of 2-½ acres of land. A large room (possibly a showroom) measured 50 x 50 (2,500 square feet) with four small rooms measuring 12 x 12 feet each. A large storage room was located at the back of the building which was thought to have stored lumber. Several storage sheds occupied the land to the north of the building. Lumber yard scales, lumber yard gates, and a railroad line also were located on the property.

The business was established in 1887 and was called Roedl, Jacobs, and Hall Lumber Yard. The company sold lumber, building materials, and fuel. The building stood on the corner of Spring and Maple. That building was ultimately razed in 1924 and was replaced by Hotel Rogers. The business moved to 108 E. Maple and resided there until sometime in 1951.

At that time, a building constructed at 114 E. Third Street (the future home of the Beaver Dam Senior Citizens Center) opened for business. The business sold coal, cement and framing lumber, nails, hardware, paint, cabinets, doorknobs, windows, and millwork. Roedl-Jacobs went out of business sometime in 1968.

At the time the building was purchased for the Beaver Dam Senior Citizens Center in 1973, Roedl-Jacobs stated they had owned the property for 30 years.

The Beaver Dam Eagles Club also had an option to purchase the property. That option expired November 20, 1972. They relinquished their option which allowed the City to purchase the property for the Beaver Dam Senior Citizens Center.

Roedl-Jacobs Lumber Yard as it looked when the building was accepted as the future site of the Beaver Dam Senior Center in 1970

Exterior buildings at back lot of Beaver Dam Senior Center—1992

Exterior buildings at back lot of Beaver Dam Senior Center—1992

Storage shed at back of the Beaver Dam Senior Center—1992

It is ironic that the current location of the Beaver Dam Senior Center at 114 E. Third Street was the location of the former Roedl-Jacobs Lumber Yard. The proposed location of the future Community Center/Senior Center at 209 S. Center Street is also the location of the former Fullerton Lumber Company—lumber company to lumber company.

The Fullerton property consists of a steel-framed retail showroom and design center which was constructed and attached to the block portion of the building in 1989 or 1990. The showroom is approximately 5,000 square feet. The block portion of the building encompasses approximately 3,700 square feet. The date of its construction is unknown. The remainder of the building is unheated storage space that was used for lumber storage by Fullerton Lumber Company. There are several small mezzanines in the interior of the building. The total square footage of the building is approximately 13,300 square feet. There are two storage buildings on the property. The acreage of the property forms into an L-shape and occupies 1.7 acres of land. The L-shape portion of the property attaches to the City of Beaver Dam parking lot.

The Dickinson Lumber Company was founded on the property in 1898. Fullerton Lumber Company purchased the property in 1946. Immediately to the right of the property at 211 S. Center was the location of the Olo Soap Company which became part of the Fullerton's property. Fullerton Lumber Company sold lumber, building supplies, and specialized in construction and remodeling. They occupied the site from 1947 until they ceased business around latter portion of 2008 or early 2009.

VISION FOR THE FUTURE

Fullerton Lumber Company, 209 South Center, donated by Charley and Gail Fakes, for the future home of the Beaver Dam Community Center/Senior Center.

And to the Future . . .

"Community Activities and Services", the new department that combined Recreation with the Senior Center provided a cost savings for the taxpayers and offered a way to continue the high level of services enjoyed by the community and surrounding areas. The transition was accomplished successfully thanks to the experience and talent of the staff involved and their willingness to think outside the box and work as a team. New ideas and modifications have served the community well and as "Your Partner for a Lifetime" the department is flourishing.

Having completed a successful state reaccreditation through WASC in 2011, the Senior Center is ready to submit an application and completed work book for National Accreditation. More and more "Baby Boomers" now participate in programs and activities. Retention of our current programs and activities is important to our older population to ensure their ability to enjoy the facility as fully as they can for as long as they can.

Thanks to a $300,000.00 contribution and the donation of the former Fullerton Building Center, a capital campaign is underway to complete a 25,000 sq. ft. Community Center. Within this project, the future of the "Senior Center" at this location holds unlimited possibilities. A more modern, spacious facility means current programs and activities will be more comfortable and additional opportunities will result in greater participation. New activities reflecting the interests of "baby boomers" can easily be added at times appropriate to the membership. The location for this new community center has broad based benefits for not only the department but the entire city and surrounding areas.

Continued involvement with other service providers and agencies, the Chamber of Commerce, the school district and local businesses provide ongoing opportunities for projects and volunteer involvement. We will continue to review our role in the community communicating our interest in partnerships wherever possible. We will also generate programs to showcase the talents of older adults and expand their role in the community.

As the population of the city ages, the numbers of people in the area who are eligible for participation increases. Discovering the interests of 'younger' older adults will be an exciting process. Our goal will be to provide programs, activities and services to everyone at the lowest possible cost.

Evonne Koeppen, Administrator, Beaver Dam Community Activities and Services

INDEX OF NAMES

Kay Appenfeldt

H   Pages Located

K   <u>Pages Located</u>

M   <u>Pages Located</u>

S   ## Pages Located

Schacht, David	6, 234
Schacht, Mary Ann	234, 235, 236
Schanen, Genny	195
Schassler, Bill	183
Schemerhorn, Dale	126
Schliesman, Frank	195
Schindel, Gilbert	5
Schinkel, Audrey	16
Schinkel, Mrs.	19
Schkirke, Elnora	97
Schley, Emerson	93
Schley, Mabel	93, 97, 102, 103, 106, 120, 121, 139, 198, 212, 235
Schliecher, Harry	64
Schmid, Dick	82
Schmidt, Bunny	94, 170
Schmidt, Eva	20, 22, 37, 50, 52
Schmidt, Gertrude	44
Schmidt, Jack	63, 101, 133, 149, 170, 198, 199, 254
Schmitt, Gertrude	88
Schmitt, Margaret	127
Schmitt, Virginia	87
Schmitz, Wayne	94, 95, 109, 119, 169, 235, 236
Schneider, Vi, Mayor	91, 151, 209
Schoeffel, Ellie	94, 110, 160, 179, 186, 187, 207, 209, 212, 213, 228 235, 239, 241, 242, 255
Schoeffel, Harvey	101, 110, 129, 149, 174, 176, 203, 204, 207, 209, 213 236, 255
Schoeffel, Katherine	18, 20
Schoenwetter, Alyce	126, 182, 184, 219, 243
Schrader, Arnold	64, 156
Schrauth, Roman	30
Schreiber, Floyd	63, 112, 142
Schroeder, Duane	126, 182
Schult, Connie	211
Schultz, Alvin	39, 64, 71, 72, 81, 82, 99, 139, 145, 149
Schultz, Christian	73, 74, 79, 82, 106
Schultz, Del	94, 95, 97, 98, 166, 169, 198, 203, 204, 207, 208, 209 212, 235, 236
Schultz, Dot	118, 119, 235
Schultz, Earl	97
Schultz, Elaine	213
Schultz, Emma	39, 145
Schultz, Lorna	128, 166, 195, 235, 238
Schultz, Mary	79

Kay Appenfeldt

W   **Pages Located**

Winning, Del, Sr.	82
Wise, Nancy	160
Wisniewski, Harry	64, 101, 103, 112
Wolff, Gloria	202
Wollin, Pearl	97, 99
Wollin, Walter	144
Woodworth, Frank	6
Woreck, Peter	133, 134
Wright, Darlene	124, 189

Y   **Pages Located**

Yagodinski, Chuck	101, 170, 198, 199
Yagodinski, Glen	64, 101, 103, 149, 170
Yaucher, Josie	24
Youngdale, Marian	189

Z   **Pages Located**

Zahn, Veronica	21
Zamora, Bob	117
Zamora, Marilyn	202
Zarling, Eugene	170
Ziebell, Mary	193
Zimmer, Ella	5
Zimmerlee, Terry	87, 170, 192, 193, 228
Zipeay, Pat	89
Zuehlke, Rachel	145